How to Start a Successful Online Business from Scratch

Franklin Fisher

Copyright © (2024) by Franklin Fisher

All rights reserved. No portion of this book may be reproduced, stored, in a retrieval system or transmitted in any format or by any means, electronical, mechanical, photocopying, recording, or otherwise, without the prior written permission of the author.

Published by Amazon KDP

Amazon.com, Inc.

P.O. Box 81226

Seattle, WA 98108-1226

United States.

Printed by Amazon KDP in the USA

Table of Contents

TABLE OF CONTENTS 3

CHAPTER 1 7

INTRODUCTION 7

   A. IMPORTANCE OF ONLINE BUSINESS IN
   TODAY'S ECONOMY 7
   B. OVERVIEW OF WHAT IT TAKES TO SUCCEED .9
   C. SETTING REALISTIC EXPECTATIONS 11

CHAPTER 2 14

UNDERSTANDING THE ONLINE BUSINESS
LANDSCAPE 14

   A. DIFFERENT TYPES OF ONLINE BUSINESSES..14
   B. MARKET RESEARCH AND NICHE
   IDENTIFICATION 18
   C. ANALYZING COMPETITORS...........................20

CHAPTER 3 24

PLANNING YOUR ONLINE BUSINESS 24

   A. DEFINING YOUR UNIQUE SELLING
   PROPOSITION (USP) 24
   B. CRAFTING A BUSINESS PLAN 27
   C. SETTING GOALS AND MILESTONES...............30

CHAPTER 4 33

BUILDING YOUR ONLINE PRESENCE 33

   A. CHOOSING THE RIGHT DOMAIN NAME 33
   B. CREATING A PROFESSIONAL WEBSITE 37

 C. Establishing Social Media Profiles 42

CHAPTER 5 48

SETTING UP YOUR E-COMMERCE INFRASTRUCTURE 48

 A. Selecting the Right E-commerce Platform 48
 B. Setting Up Payment Gateways 53
 C. Implementing Secure Checkout Processes 59

CHAPTER 6 65

MARKETING AND PROMOTIONS 65

 A. Developing a Marketing Strategy 65
 B. Content Marketing and SEO 69
 C. Social Media Marketing 73
 D. Email Marketing 77

CHAPTER 7 83

MANAGING FINANCES AND OPERATIONS 83

 A. Budgeting and Financial Planning 83
 B. Inventory Management 89
 C. Fulfillment and Shipping 95

CHAPTER 8 102

SCALING YOUR ONLINE BUSINESS 102

 A. Identifying Growth Opportunities 102
 B. Hiring and Outsourcing 107
 C. Automating Processes 112

CHAPTER 9 121

HANDLING CHALLENGES AND RISKS 121

A. Dealing with Competition 121
B. Managing Customer Service 125
C. Overcoming Financial Hurdles 130

CHAPTER 10 135

MEASURING SUCCESS AND CONTINUOUS IMPROVEMENT 135

A. Key Performance Indicators (KPIs) 135
B. Analyzing Data and Making Informed Decisions 139
C. Adapting to Market Changes 143

CHAPTER 11 148

CONCLUSION 148

A. Recap of Key Points 148
B. Encouragement and Final Words of Advice 151

CHAPTER 12 155

ADDITIONAL RESOURCES 155

A. Recommended Tools and Software 155
B. Further Reading and References 161
C. Glossary of Terms 164

Chapter 1

Introduction

In today's digital age, the landscape of business has undergone a significant transformation. The advent of the internet has revolutionized the way we conduct commerce, enabling entrepreneurs to reach customers globally from the comfort of their own homes. The rise of online businesses has not only reshaped traditional industries but has also created entirely new avenues for economic growth and innovation. In this comprehensive guide, we will explore the ins and outs of starting a successful online business from scratch. From understanding the importance of online commerce in today's economy to setting realistic expectations and everything in between, this guide aims to provide aspiring entrepreneurs with the knowledge and tools they need to thrive in the digital marketplace.

A. Importance of Online Business in Today's Economy

The importance of online business in today's economy cannot be overstated. With the widespread adoption of internet-connected devices and the increasing prevalence of e-commerce platforms, consumers have come to expect the convenience of shopping online for a wide range of products and services. From groceries to electronics, clothing to household goods, almost anything can be purchased with just a few clicks or taps.

One of the key advantages of online business is its ability to reach a global audience. Unlike traditional brick-and-mortar stores limited by geographical location, online businesses have the potential to attract customers from all corners of the globe. This level of accessibility not only expands the customer base but also opens up opportunities for growth and expansion into new markets.

Moreover, online business offers unparalleled flexibility and scalability. With minimal overhead costs compared to physical storefronts, entrepreneurs can launch and operate an online business with relatively low financial investment. Additionally, the digital nature of online commerce allows for easy scalability, enabling businesses to quickly adapt to changes in demand and seize new opportunities for growth.

Furthermore, the COVID-19 pandemic has underscored the importance of online business resilience. During lockdowns and social distancing measures, many brick-and-mortar businesses were forced to close their doors temporarily, while online businesses continued to operate and even thrive in some cases. This shift in consumer behavior towards online shopping has accelerated the digital transformation of industries worldwide, making it more crucial than ever for businesses to establish a strong online presence.

In summary, online business plays a vital role in driving economic growth, fostering innovation, and meeting the evolving needs of consumers in today's interconnected world.

B. Overview of What it Takes to Succeed

While the allure of starting an online business may be enticing, achieving success in the digital marketplace requires more than just a good idea and a website. It demands dedication, perseverance, and a strategic approach to building and growing a sustainable business.

First and foremost, successful online entrepreneurs possess a clear vision and a deep understanding of their target market. They identify unmet needs or pain points within their niche and develop innovative solutions to address them. This customer-centric approach forms the foundation of a successful business, ensuring that products or services resonate with the intended audience and deliver tangible value.

Additionally, successful online businesses prioritize quality and customer satisfaction above all else. They invest in creating compelling products or services that stand out from the competition and consistently exceed customer expectations. By delivering exceptional value and fostering positive customer experiences, businesses can build loyalty and establish a strong reputation in the marketplace.

Furthermore, successful online entrepreneurs embrace continuous learning and adaptation. They stay informed about industry trends, emerging technologies, and evolving consumer preferences, allowing them to anticipate changes and pivot their strategies accordingly. Whether it's experimenting with new marketing channels, optimizing website design, or refining product offerings, successful businesses are always seeking ways to innovate and stay ahead of the curve.

Finally, success in the world of online business requires resilience and determination. Building a successful business takes time, and setbacks and challenges are inevitable along the way. However, successful entrepreneurs view these obstacles as opportunities for growth and learning, persisting in the face of adversity and remaining focused on their long-term goals.

In summary, succeeding in the online business requires a combination of vision, customer focus, quality, adaptability, and resilience.

C. Setting Realistic Expectations

While the potential rewards of starting an online business are undoubtedly appealing, it's essential for aspiring entrepreneurs to set realistic expectations from the outset. Building a successful online business takes time, effort, and patience, and success rarely happens overnight.

First and foremost, aspiring entrepreneurs must recognize that success in the online business requires hard work and dedication. While the internet has made it easier than ever to start a business, competition in the digital marketplace is fierce, and standing out requires a considerable investment of time and effort. From market research and product development to marketing and customer acquisition, building a successful online business demands relentless focus and perseverance.

Moreover, aspiring entrepreneurs must understand that success is not guaranteed and that failure is a natural part of the entrepreneurial journey. Not every idea will resonate with consumers, and not every venture will yield the desired results. However, failure is not the end but rather an opportunity to learn, grow, and iterate on ideas. By embracing failure as a stepping stone to success and maintaining a positive mindset, aspiring entrepreneurs can navigate the ups and downs of the entrepreneurial journey with resilience and determination.

Furthermore, setting realistic financial expectations is crucial for long-term success. While online businesses have the potential for significant profitability, it's essential to recognize that generating sustainable revenue takes time. In the early stages, most businesses operate at a loss as they invest in product development, marketing, and infrastructure. As such, aspiring entrepreneurs should be prepared to weather the initial financial challenges and focus on building a solid foundation for future growth.

In summary, setting realistic expectations is essential for aspiring entrepreneurs embarking on the journey of starting an online business. By recognizing the challenges, embracing failure as a learning opportunity, and maintaining a long-term perspective, entrepreneurs can increase their chances of success in the competitive world of online commerce.

Chapter 2

Understanding the Online Business Landscape

In today's digital age, the online business landscape offers a multitude of opportunities for entrepreneurs to launch and grow successful ventures. From e-commerce stores and digital marketplaces to content-based platforms and subscription services, the diversity of online business models allows entrepreneurs to tailor their offerings to specific market segments and consumer preferences. In this section, we will explore the different types of online businesses, the importance of market research and niche identification, and strategies for analyzing competitors to gain a competitive edge.

A. Different Types of Online Businesses

1. **E-commerce Stores:** E-commerce stores are online platforms that sell physical products directly to consumers. These businesses range

from small, independent boutiques to large-scale retailers like Amazon and Walmart. E-commerce stores may specialize in specific product categories, such as fashion, electronics, or home goods, or offer a wide range of products across multiple categories.

2. **Digital Products and Services:** Digital products and services encompass a broad range of offerings, including e-books, online courses, software applications, digital downloads, and subscription-based services. These businesses leverage digital technology to deliver intangible goods or services to customers, often with minimal overhead costs and scalable revenue potential.

3. **Affiliate Marketing:** Affiliate marketing involves promoting other companies' products or services and earning a commission for each sale or referral generated through your promotional efforts. Affiliates typically earn a percentage of the sale price or a fixed commission for each referral, making it a popular choice for entrepreneurs looking to monetize their online presence without the

hassle of managing inventory or customer support.
4. **Content-based Platforms:** Content-based platforms, such as blogs, vlogs, podcasts, and social media channels, generate revenue through advertising, sponsorships, affiliate marketing, and direct monetization methods like paid subscriptions or donations. These businesses focus on creating valuable content that attracts and engages audiences, ultimately driving traffic and revenue through various monetization strategies.
5. **Software as a Service (SaaS):** SaaS businesses offer cloud-based software solutions that customers can access and use on a subscription basis. These businesses cater to a wide range of industries and use cases, providing tools and services for everything from project management and customer relationship management to email marketing and accounting.
6. **Freelancing and Consulting:** Freelancing and consulting businesses leverage specialized skills and expertise to provide services to clients on a freelance or contract basis. These businesses may offer

services such as graphic design, web development, digital marketing, writing, consulting, and coaching, among others.

7. **Dropshipping**: Dropshipping is a retail fulfillment method where a store sells products to customers without holding inventory. Instead, the store purchases products from a third party and ships them directly to the customer. Dropshipping businesses benefit from low startup costs, as they don't need to invest in inventory upfront, but they face challenges related to product quality, shipping times, and customer satisfaction.

8. **Subscription Box Services:** Subscription box services deliver curated collections of products to customers on a recurring basis, typically monthly or quarterly. These businesses appeal to consumers looking for convenience, novelty, and personalized recommendations, offering everything from beauty and wellness products to gourmet food and pet supplies.

9. **Online Marketplaces:** Online marketplaces connect buyers and sellers in a virtual marketplace,

facilitating transactions between parties. Marketplaces may focus on specific product categories, such as handmade goods, vintage items, or digital downloads, or offer a wide range of products and services across multiple categories.
10. **Drop Servicing:** Drop servicing is a business model similar to dropshipping, but instead of selling physical products, entrepreneurs offer services sourced from third-party providers to clients. Drop servicing businesses act as intermediaries, outsourcing tasks such as graphic design, writing, or digital marketing to freelancers or agencies and charging a markup for their services.

B. Market Research and Niche Identification

Before launching an online business, it's crucial to conduct thorough market research and identify a profitable niche. Market research involves gathering and analyzing data about your target market, industry trends, customer preferences, and competitive landscape to inform your business strategy and decision-making process.

1. **Identify Market Trends:** Start by researching industry trends, market demand, and emerging opportunities within your niche. Look for areas of growth and innovation, as well as potential challenges or obstacles that may impact your business's success.
2. **Define Your Target Audience:** Determine who your ideal customers are and what their needs, preferences, and pain points are. Develop detailed buyer personas to understand your target audience's demographics, psychographics, and purchasing behavior, allowing you to tailor your products or services to meet their specific needs.
3. **Assess Market Size and Potential:** Evaluate the size and potential of your target market to gauge the demand for your products or services. Look for market gaps or underserved segments that present opportunities for differentiation and growth.
4. **Analyze Competitors:** Study your competitors to understand their strengths, weaknesses, and market positioning. Identify gaps in their

offerings, areas where you can differentiate your business, and opportunities for innovation and improvement.
5. **Conduct Keyword Research:** Use keyword research tools to identify relevant search terms and phrases related to your niche. This will help you understand what topics and keywords your target audience is searching for online, allowing you to optimize your website content, marketing campaigns, and SEO strategy accordingly.
6. **Validate Your Idea:** Test your business idea and product concept with potential customers through surveys, focus groups, or beta testing. Gather feedback, validate demand, and iterate on your offerings based on customer input to ensure product-market fit.

C. Analyzing Competitors

Competitive analysis is a critical component of market research, helping you identify key competitors, assess their strengths and weaknesses, and identify opportunities for differentiation and competitive advantage. By understanding your competitors' strategies, positioning, and performance, you can make more informed decisions and develop a strategy to outmaneuver them in the marketplace.

1. **Identify Key Competitors:** Start by identifying your main competitors within your niche or industry. Look for businesses that offer similar products or services, target the same audience, or operate in the same geographic region.
2. **Analyze Competitor Websites:** Visit your competitors' websites and analyze their design, layout, messaging, and user experience. Pay attention to their product offerings, pricing, promotions, and value propositions to understand how they position themselves in the market and attract customers.
3. **Assess Marketing Strategies:** Study your competitors' marketing strategies and channels to identify which tactics are most effective in reaching and engaging their target audience. Look for opportunities to emulate successful strategies or differentiate your business by targeting underserved channels or niches.

4. **Evaluate Product Offerings:** Evaluate your competitors' product offerings in terms of quality, features, pricing, and value proposition. Identify gaps or shortcomings in their offerings that you can address with your own products or services, and look for opportunities to innovate and differentiate.
5. **Analyze Customer Reviews and Feedback:** Read customer reviews and feedback about your competitors' products or services to identify common pain points, complaints, and areas for improvement. Use this information to inform your own product development and customer service strategy and address unmet needs or concerns in the market.
6. **Monitor Social Media and Online Presence:** Monitor your competitors' social media profiles, online forums, and review sites to gauge customer sentiment, track industry trends, and stay updated on their latest developments and announcements. Look for opportunities to engage with their audience, participate in relevant conversations, and showcase your unique value proposition.

7. **SWOT Analysis:** Conduct a SWOT analysis (Strengths, Weaknesses, Opportunities, Threats) to assess your competitors' overall competitive position and identify strategic insights and recommendations

Chapter 3

Planning Your Online Business

Planning is a crucial step in starting any business, and online ventures are no exception. In this section, we'll delve into the key aspects of planning your online business, including defining your Unique Selling Proposition (USP), crafting a business plan, and setting goals and milestones to guide your journey to success.

A. Defining Your Unique Selling Proposition (USP)

Your Unique Selling Proposition (USP) is what sets your business apart from the competition and makes it unique in the eyes of your target audience. It's the reason why customers should choose your products or services over those offered by your competitors. Defining your USP is essential for creating a strong brand identity, attracting customers, and building a loyal customer base. Here are some steps to help you define your USP:

1. **Identify Your Strengths:** Start by identifying the unique strengths, capabilities, and assets that your business brings to the table. This could include factors such as superior product quality, exceptional customer service, innovative features or technology, competitive pricing, or exclusive partnerships with suppliers.
2. **Understand Your Target Audience:** Gain a deep understanding of your target audience's needs, preferences, and pain points. What problems are they trying to solve, and how can your products or services address those needs better than your competitors? By understanding your audience's motivations and desires, you can tailor your USP to resonate with their interests and preferences.
3. **Analyze the Competition:** Research your competitors to understand their offerings, strengths, and weaknesses. Identify gaps or shortcomings in the market that you can capitalize on with your own unique value proposition. Look for opportunities to differentiate your business by offering something that your competitors don't or by

providing a better solution to common customer problems.

4. **Communicate Your USP Effectively:** Once you've defined your USP, it's essential to communicate it effectively to your target audience. Incorporate your USP into your branding, messaging, marketing materials, and website copy to ensure consistency and clarity. Highlight the benefits of choosing your products or services and clearly articulate what makes your business unique and compelling.

5. **Continuously Evolve and Adapt:** The business landscape is constantly evolving, and your USP may need to evolve along with it. Stay informed about industry trends, emerging technologies, and changes in consumer preferences, and be prepared to adapt your USP accordingly. Continuously seek feedback from customers and monitor the competitive landscape to ensure that your USP remains relevant and compelling over time.

B. Crafting a Business Plan

A business plan is a roadmap that outlines your business goals, strategies, and action plans for achieving success. It serves as a blueprint for your business, providing direction, clarity, and structure to your entrepreneurial journey. Here are the key components of a comprehensive business plan:

1. **Executive Summary:** Summarize the key aspects of your business plan, including your business concept, target market, competitive analysis, marketing strategy, financial projections, and funding requirements.
2. **Business Description:** Provide an overview of your business concept, mission, vision, and values. Describe the products or services you plan to offer, your target market, and your unique selling proposition (USP).
3. **Market Analysis:** Conduct a thorough analysis of your target market, industry trends, customer demographics, and competitive landscape. Identify opportunities, threats, strengths, and weaknesses in

the market that may impact your business's success.
4. **Marketing and Sales Strategy:** Outline your marketing and sales strategies for acquiring and retaining customers. Describe how you plan to reach your target audience, promote your products or services, generate leads, and convert prospects into customers. Include details about your pricing strategy, distribution channels, and sales forecasts.
5. **Operations and Management:** Describe the operational and organizational structure of your business, including roles and responsibilities, staffing requirements, and processes for day-to-day operations. Identify any technology, equipment, or infrastructure needed to support your business operations.
6. **Financial Projections:** Provide detailed financial projections for your business, including sales forecasts, revenue projections, expense estimates, and cash flow analysis. Include a break-even analysis and projected income statement, balance sheet, and cash flow statement for the first few years of operation.

7. **Funding Requirements:** If you require external funding to launch or grow your business, outline your funding requirements and potential sources of financing. This may include equity investment, loans, grants, or crowdfunding campaigns. Specify how the funds will be used and the expected return on investment for investors or lenders.
8. **Risk Management:** Identify potential risks and challenges that may impact your business's success and outline strategies for mitigating and managing these risks. This may include market risks, competitive threats, regulatory compliance issues, or operational challenges.
9. **Implementation Plan:** Develop a detailed implementation plan that outlines the steps and milestones for launching and growing your business. Include timelines, deadlines, and responsibilities for each task, and set measurable goals and objectives to track progress and performance.
10. **Monitoring and Evaluation:** Establish metrics and key performance indicators (KPIs) to measure the success of your business and track progress towards your

goals. Regularly monitor and evaluate your performance against these metrics, and make adjustments to your strategy as needed to optimize results.

C. Setting Goals and Milestones

Setting clear, measurable goals and milestones is essential for guiding your business's growth and progress. Goals provide direction and focus, while milestones help break down larger objectives into smaller, achievable steps. Here are some tips for setting effective goals and milestones for your online business:

1. **Define Specific Objectives:** Start by defining specific, actionable goals that align with your business objectives and priorities. Whether it's increasing sales, expanding market reach, improving customer satisfaction, or launching a new product or service, make sure your goals are clear, measurable, and achievable within a reasonable timeframe.
2. **Set Measurable Targets:** Establish key performance indicators (KPIs)

and metrics to measure progress towards your goals. This could include metrics such as sales revenue, website traffic, conversion rates, customer acquisition cost, customer lifetime value, or social media engagement. By setting measurable targets, you can track your performance and identify areas for improvement.
3. **Break Goals into Milestones:** Break down larger goals into smaller, manageable milestones or objectives that can be achieved incrementally. This allows you to track progress more effectively and celebrate small wins along the way, keeping your team motivated and focused on achieving the larger goal.
4. **Prioritize and Allocate Resources:** Prioritize your goals based on their importance and urgency, and allocate resources, time, and budget accordingly. Focus on high-impact initiatives that align with your business strategy and have the potential to drive significant results.
5. **Create Action Plans:** Develop detailed action plans outlining the specific tasks, activities, and deadlines required to achieve each

goal and milestone. Assign responsibilities to team members and set clear expectations for accountability and performance.
6. **Review and Adjust as Needed:** Regularly review your progress towards your goals and milestones, and make adjustments to your strategy as needed based on performance data and changing market conditions. Be flexible and adaptive, and don't be afraid to revise your goals or action plans if circumstances warrant it.
7. **Celebrate Achievements:** Celebrate achievements and milestones along the way to acknowledge the hard work and dedication of your team. Recognize and reward progress towards goals, and use these moments to build morale and momentum for future success.

By defining your Unique Selling Proposition (USP), crafting a comprehensive business plan, and setting clear goals and milestones, you can lay the foundation for a successful online business that stands out in the competitive marketplace.

Chapter 4

Building Your Online Presence

In today's digital age, having a strong online presence is essential for businesses of all sizes. A well-established online presence not only helps businesses reach and engage with their target audience but also builds credibility, trust, and brand recognition. In this section, we'll explore the key components of building your online presence, including choosing the right domain name, creating a professional website, and establishing social media profiles to connect with your audience effectively.

A. Choosing the Right Domain Name

Your domain name is your online identity and plays a crucial role in shaping your brand's perception and visibility on the internet. It's the web address that users type into their browsers to access your website, so choosing the right domain name is essential for establishing a memorable and recognizable online presence. Here are some tips for choosing the right domain name for your business:

1. **Keep it Short and Simple:** Choose a domain name that is short, easy to spell, and easy to remember. Avoid using hyphens, numbers, or special characters that can confuse users and make your domain name harder to type or remember.
2. **Reflect Your Brand:** Your domain name should reflect your brand identity and convey the essence of your business. Ideally, it should include your brand name or a relevant keyword that describes your products or services. Make sure it's relevant, meaningful, and aligns with your brand's values and positioning.
3. **Use Keywords Strategically:** Incorporate relevant keywords into your domain name to improve search engine visibility and attract organic traffic. Research keywords related to your industry, niche, or target audience and incorporate them naturally into your domain name without sacrificing readability or brand identity.

4. **Choose the Right Domain Extension:** Consider the top-level domain (TLD) extension that best suits your business and target audience. While .com is the most popular and widely recognized TLD, other options like .net, .org, .co, or country-specific extensions like .uk or .ca may be more suitable depending on your business's location or industry.
5. **Check Availability and Trademarks:** Before registering a domain name, conduct a thorough search to ensure that it's available and not already registered by another party. Check for trademarks or existing businesses with similar names to avoid potential legal issues. Use domain registration platforms or WHOIS databases to check domain availability and ownership.
6. **Consider Brand Protection:** Consider registering variations or misspellings of your domain name to prevent competitors or malicious actors from capitalizing on your brand name or diverting traffic to their websites. Registering multiple domain extensions or variations can help protect your brand and ensure

consistent branding across different channels.
7. **Think Long-Term:** Choose a domain name that will stand the test of time and grow with your business. Avoid trendy or overly niche-specific names that may become outdated or limiting as your business evolves. Think long-term and choose a domain name that is timeless, versatile, and scalable.
8. **Seek Feedback:** Once you've narrowed down your options, seek feedback from colleagues, friends, or industry peers to get their input and perspective on your domain name choices. Consider their feedback and insights to make an informed decision that aligns with your brand and business goals.

In summary, choosing the right domain name is a critical step in building your online presence and establishing your brand identity on the internet. Take the time to research, brainstorm, and choose a domain name that reflects your brand, resonates with your target audience, and sets you up for long-term success.

B. Creating a Professional Website

Your website serves as the online hub for your business and is often the first point of contact between your brand and potential customers. A professional website not only showcases your products or services but also provides valuable information, builds trust, and drives conversions. Here are the key steps to creating a professional website for your business:

1. **Define Your Objectives:** Start by defining the objectives and goals of your website. What do you want to achieve with your website? Is it to generate leads, sell products, provide information, or build brand awareness? Clarifying your objectives will help guide the design and development process and ensure that your website aligns with your business goals.
2. **Choose the Right Platform:** Select a website platform or content management system (CMS) that meets your needs and technical requirements. Popular options include WordPress, Shopify, Wix,

Squarespace, and Magento, each offering different features, flexibility, and customization options. Consider factors such as ease of use, scalability, customization options, and integration capabilities when choosing a platform for your website.
3. **Select a Professional Design:** Choose a professional design theme or template that reflects your brand identity and appeals to your target audience. Opt for clean, modern designs with intuitive navigation, clear calls-to-action, and mobile responsiveness to provide an optimal user experience across devices and screen sizes. Customize the design to incorporate your brand colors, fonts, imagery, and logo for a cohesive and branded look.
4. **Create Compelling Content:** Develop high-quality content that engages and informs your website visitors. This includes compelling copywriting, captivating images, informative videos, and interactive elements that showcase your products or services and highlight their benefits and features. Use persuasive language and storytelling techniques

to connect with your audience emotionally and drive action.

5. **Optimize for Search Engines (SEO):** Implement search engine optimization (SEO) best practices to improve your website's visibility and ranking in search engine results. This includes optimizing on-page elements such as meta titles, descriptions, headings, and image alt tags, as well as creating high-quality, relevant content that targets keywords and addresses user intent. Focus on providing value to users and adhering to SEO guidelines to attract organic traffic and increase your website's visibility in search results.

6. **Incorporate Conversion Optimization:** Design your website with conversion optimization in mind to encourage visitors to take desired actions, such as making a purchase, filling out a contact form, or subscribing to your newsletter. Use clear calls-to-action, strategically placed buttons, and persuasive messaging to guide users through the conversion funnel and make it easy for them to take action.

7. **Ensure Mobile-Friendliness:** With the increasing use of mobile devices

for browsing the internet, it's essential to ensure that your website is mobile-friendly and optimized for mobile users. Choose a responsive design that adapts to different screen sizes and resolutions, and test your website across various devices and browsers to ensure a seamless and consistent user experience.

8. **Implement Security Measures:** Protect your website and sensitive customer data by implementing robust security measures and protocols. Use SSL encryption to secure data transmission, install security plugins or software to detect and prevent malware and cyber attacks, and regularly update your website's software, plugins, and themes to patch security vulnerabilities and stay protected against emerging threats.

9. **Test and Iterate:** Before launching your website, thoroughly test its functionality, usability, and performance across different devices and browsers. Conduct usability testing with real users to identify any usability issues or friction points and make necessary adjustments. Monitor website analytics and user feedback

post-launch to track performance, identify areas for improvement, and iterate on your website to enhance the user experience and achieve your business goals.
10. **Provide Ongoing Maintenance and Support:** Once your website is live, provide ongoing maintenance, updates, and support to ensure its continued performance, security, and relevance. Regularly update content, monitor website analytics, and address any technical issues or customer inquiries promptly to maintain a positive user experience and maximize the impact of your online presence.

In summary, creating a professional website is essential for establishing a strong online presence and connecting with your target audience effectively. By following these steps and implementing best practices for website design, content creation, search engine optimization, and user experience, you can create a professional website that showcases your brand, engages your audience, and drives conversions.

C. Establishing Social Media Profiles

In addition to your website, social media platforms provide valuable channels for building and expanding your online presence, engaging with your audience, and driving traffic to your website. Establishing social media profiles allows you to connect with potential customers, showcase your products or services, and cultivate a community around your brand. Here's how to effectively establish and leverage social media profiles for your business:

1. **Choose the Right Platforms:** Start by identifying the social media platforms that are most relevant to your target audience and align with your business objectives. Popular platforms include Facebook, Instagram, Twitter, LinkedIn, Pinterest, YouTube, and TikTok, each catering to different demographics, interests, and content formats. Research your target audience's preferences and behavior on social media to determine which platforms are best suited for reaching and engaging with them.

2. **Create Branded Profiles:** Set up branded profiles on selected social media platforms that reflect your brand identity and messaging consistently. Use your logo, brand colors, and imagery to create a cohesive and recognizable presence across all social media channels. Complete your profile information, including your business name, bio, website URL, and contact information, to provide users with essential information about your business and encourage engagement.
3. **Develop a Content Strategy:** Develop a content strategy that aligns with your brand identity, target audience, and business goals. Create a content calendar outlining the types of content you'll publish, the topics you'll cover, and the frequency of posting. Mix up your content mix with a variety of formats, including text-based posts, images, videos, infographics, polls, and user-generated content, to keep your audience engaged and entertained.
4. **Engage with Your Audience:** Actively engage with your audience on social media by responding to comments, messages, and mentions

promptly. Foster conversations, ask questions, and encourage user-generated content to encourage interaction and build a sense of community around your brand. Show appreciation for your followers' support, acknowledge their feedback, and address any concerns or inquiries professionally and empathetically.
5. **Use Hashtags Strategically:** Incorporate relevant hashtags into your social media posts to increase visibility and reach a broader audience. Research popular and trending hashtags related to your industry, niche, or target audience, and include them strategically in your posts to improve discoverability and engagement. Create branded hashtags to encourage user-generated content and foster community participation around your brand.
6. **Leverage Visual Content:** Visual content performs exceptionally well on social media and is more likely to capture users' attention and drive engagement. Use high-quality images, videos, and graphics to make your posts visually appealing and stand out in users' feeds. Experiment with different types of visual content,

such as product photos, behind-the-scenes shots, infographics, and animations, to keep your feed fresh and engaging.

7. **Monitor Performance and Analytics:** Regularly monitor the performance of your social media profiles and track key metrics and analytics to evaluate your effectiveness and optimize your strategy. Use social media analytics tools and platforms to measure engagement, reach, impressions, click-through rates, conversion rates, and other relevant metrics. Identify top-performing content, audience demographics, and trends to inform future content strategy and campaign optimization.

8. **Collaborate with Influencers and Partners:** Partner with influencers, brand ambassadors, or complementary businesses to amplify your reach and exposure on social media. Identify influencers or partners whose audience aligns with your target demographic and collaborate on sponsored content, co-branded campaigns, or joint promotions to expand your reach and attract new followers and customers.

9. **Run Paid Advertising Campaigns:** Consider running paid advertising campaigns on social media platforms to increase visibility, reach, and engagement with your target audience. Experiment with different ad formats, targeting options, and campaign objectives to maximize your return on investment (ROI) and achieve your business goals. Set clear objectives, define your target audience, and allocate your budget effectively to optimize campaign performance and drive results.
10. **Stay Updated and Adapt:** The social media landscape is constantly evolving, with new features, trends, and algorithms emerging regularly. Stay updated on the latest social media trends, best practices, and platform updates to adapt your strategy accordingly and capitalize on new opportunities. Experiment with new content formats, features, and strategies to keep your social media presence fresh, relevant, and engaging for your audience.

In summary, establishing social media profiles is essential for building your online presence, connecting with your audience, and driving traffic and engagement to your website. By choosing the right platforms, creating compelling content, engaging with your audience, and leveraging analytics and insights, you can effectively leverage social media to achieve your business goals and grow your brand online.

Chapter 5

Setting Up Your E-commerce Infrastructure

Setting up a robust e-commerce infrastructure is essential for launching and running a successful online store. From selecting the right e-commerce platform to implementing secure payment gateways and checkout processes, every aspect of your infrastructure plays a crucial role in providing a seamless and secure shopping experience for your customers. In this comprehensive guide, we'll explore the key steps involved in setting up your e-commerce infrastructure, including selecting the right e-commerce platform, setting up payment gateways, and implementing secure checkout processes to protect customer data and facilitate smooth transactions.

A. Selecting the Right E-commerce Platform

Choosing the right e-commerce platform is the foundation of your online store and can significantly impact its success. With numerous options available in the market, ranging from hosted solutions to open-source platforms, it's essential to evaluate your business needs, budget, and technical requirements before making a decision. Here's how to select the right e-commerce platform for your business:

1. **Define Your Requirements:** Start by identifying your business requirements, including your product catalog size, sales volume, scalability needs, customization requirements, and budget constraints. Determine whether you need basic features for a small boutique store or advanced functionality for a large-scale enterprise operation.
2. **Consider Hosting Options:** Decide whether you prefer a hosted solution, where the e-commerce platform hosts your website and manages technical aspects like server maintenance and security updates, or a self-hosted solution, where you have more control and flexibility but also more responsibility for technical maintenance and security.
3. **Evaluate Features and Functionality:** Compare the features and functionality offered by different e-commerce platforms to ensure they

align with your business needs and goals. Look for essential features such as product management, inventory tracking, order management, payment processing, shipping integration, and marketing tools. Consider additional features like multi-channel selling, SEO optimization, analytics, and reporting to support your growth and expansion.

4. **Assess Customization Options:** Evaluate the level of customization and flexibility offered by each e-commerce platform to tailor your store to your brand identity and unique requirements. Look for platforms that allow you to customize themes, templates, layouts, and design elements without requiring advanced coding skills. Consider whether you need access to a marketplace of third-party apps and extensions to add additional functionality and integrations as your business grows.

5. **Review Security Measures:** Prioritize security when evaluating e-commerce platforms to protect your customers' sensitive data and ensure compliance with industry standards

and regulations. Look for platforms that offer built-in security features such as SSL encryption, PCI compliance, fraud prevention tools, and regular security updates. Consider whether the platform integrates with reputable payment gateways and supports secure checkout processes to safeguard customer transactions.

6. **Analyze Pricing and Costs:** Compare pricing plans and subscription models offered by different e-commerce platforms to find one that fits within your budget and offers the best value for your money. Consider factors such as monthly fees, transaction fees, processing fees, add-on costs for premium features or support, and scalability options as your business grows.

7. **Read Reviews and Testimonials:** Research customer reviews, testimonials, and case studies to learn about other merchants' experiences with different e-commerce platforms. Look for feedback on ease of use, reliability, customer support, performance, and overall satisfaction to make an informed decision.

Consider joining online communities, forums, or user groups to ask questions, share experiences, and get recommendations from fellow e-commerce entrepreneurs.
8. **Take Advantage of Free Trials:** Many e-commerce platforms offer free trials or demo versions that allow you to test-drive the platform and explore its features and functionality before making a commitment. Take advantage of these opportunities to get hands-on experience with the platform, experiment with different settings and configurations, and assess its suitability for your business needs.
9. **Plan for Growth and Scalability:** Choose an e-commerce platform that can accommodate your business's growth and scalability needs over time. Look for platforms that offer flexible pricing plans, scalable infrastructure, and built-in features or integrations to support expansion into new markets, channels, and product lines as your business grows.
10. **Seek Expert Advice:** If you're unsure about which e-commerce platform is right for your business, consider seeking expert advice from e-

commerce consultants, web developers, or digital agencies with experience in e-commerce website development and platform selection. They can offer insights, recommendations, and best practices based on your specific requirements and industry expertise.

In summary, selecting the right e-commerce platform is a critical decision that can significantly impact the success and growth of your online store. By carefully evaluating your business requirements, considering key factors such as features, customization options, security, pricing, and scalability, and seeking expert advice when needed, you can choose an e-commerce platform that meets your needs and sets your business up for success.

B. Setting Up Payment Gateways

Payment gateways are essential components of your e-commerce infrastructure that facilitate secure online transactions and enable customers to make purchases on your website. Setting up payment gateways involves integrating third-party payment processing services with your e-commerce platform to accept various payment methods, such as credit cards, debit cards, digital wallets, and alternative payment options. Here's how to set up payment gateways for your online store:

1. **Choose Compatible Payment Gateways:** Research and choose payment gateways that are compatible with your e-commerce platform and support the payment methods preferred by your target audience. Popular payment gateways include PayPal, Stripe, Square, Authorize.Net, Braintree, and 2Checkout, among others. Consider factors such as transaction fees, processing rates, supported currencies, security features, and ease of integration when selecting payment gateways for your online store.
2. **Create Merchant Accounts:** Sign up for merchant accounts with selected payment gateways to enable payment processing for your online store. Merchant accounts are required to accept payments and receive funds from customer transactions. Provide the necessary information and documentation, such as business details, banking information, tax identification

numbers, and legal documentation, to create merchant accounts with your chosen payment gateways.

3. **Configure Payment Settings:** Configure payment settings and preferences within your e-commerce platform to integrate payment gateways and enable payment processing on your website. Depending on your platform, you may need to install and configure payment gateway plugins or extensions, enter API credentials, set up payment methods, and configure checkout settings to enable seamless payment processing for customers.

4. **Test Payment Integration:** Test payment integration and processing to ensure that payment gateways are set up correctly and functioning as expected. Conduct test transactions using different payment methods, such as credit cards, debit cards, and digital wallets, to verify that payments are processed successfully, funds are transferred to your merchant account, and orders are recorded accurately in your e-commerce platform.

5. **Implement Security Measures:** Implement security measures to protect sensitive customer data and ensure secure transactions throughout the payment process. Ensure that your website is SSL encrypted to encrypt data transmission between the

customer's browser and your server, preventing unauthorized access to payment information. Follow PCI DSS (Payment Card Industry Data Security Standard) compliance requirements and best practices to secure payment gateways, protect customer data, and prevent fraud.

6. **Offer Multiple Payment Options:** Provide customers with multiple payment options to accommodate their preferences and increase conversion rates. Offer popular payment methods such as credit cards (Visa, Mastercard, American Express), debit cards, PayPal, Apple Pay, Google Pay, and other digital wallets. Consider supporting alternative payment methods and local payment options to cater to diverse customer preferences and international audiences.

7. **Streamline Checkout Process:** Streamline the checkout process to minimize friction and reduce cart abandonment rates. Optimize your checkout flow by eliminating unnecessary steps, reducing form fields, providing guest checkout options, offering one-click or saved payment methods, and displaying clear progress indicators. Provide real-time order summaries, shipping options, and transparent pricing to instill trust and confidence in customers and encourage them to complete their purchases.

8. **Monitor Payment Performance:** Monitor payment performance and analytics to track transaction metrics, identify trends, and optimize payment processes for better performance and efficiency. Use payment gateway dashboards, reports, and analytics tools to monitor transaction volumes, approval rates, decline rates, chargeback ratios, and other key performance indicators. Analyze transaction data to identify opportunities for improvement, address issues proactively, and optimize payment strategies to maximize revenue and customer satisfaction.

9. **Ensure Compliance:** Ensure compliance with relevant regulations, laws, and industry standards governing payment processing and data security. Stay informed about updates to payment regulations, privacy laws, and security standards, such as GDPR (General Data Protection Regulation) and PSD2 (Payment Services Directive 2), and ensure that your payment processes adhere to these requirements. Work with legal and compliance experts to ensure that your payment gateway setup and practices comply with applicable regulations and standards to avoid potential legal and financial consequences.

10. **Provide Support and Assistance:** Offer customer support and assistance to

address any payment-related inquiries, issues, or concerns that customers may have. Provide clear contact information, FAQs, and help documentation on your website to assist customers with payment-related questions or troubleshooting. Train your support team to handle payment inquiries professionally and efficiently, and provide timely responses and resolutions to ensure a positive customer experience throughout the payment process.

In summary, setting up payment gateways is a critical aspect of establishing your e-commerce infrastructure and facilitating secure online transactions for your customers. By choosing compatible payment gateways, creating merchant accounts, configuring payment settings, implementing security measures, offering multiple payment options, streamlining the checkout process, monitoring payment performance, ensuring compliance, and providing support and assistance, you can set up payment gateways effectively and provide a seamless and secure payment experience for your online store customers.

C. Implementing Secure Checkout Processes

Implementing secure checkout processes is essential for protecting customer data, preventing fraud, and building trust and confidence in your e-commerce store. A secure checkout process ensures that sensitive information, such as payment details and personal data, is encrypted and transmitted securely to prevent unauthorized access or interception by third parties. Here's how to implement secure checkout processes for your online store:

1. **Use SSL Encryption:** Secure your checkout process with SSL (Secure Sockets Layer) encryption to encrypt data transmission between the customer's browser and your server. SSL encryption protects sensitive information, such as credit card numbers, passwords, and personal data, from being intercepted or accessed by hackers or malicious actors. Obtain an SSL certificate from a trusted certificate authority and configure your website to use HTTPS protocol to encrypt data and display a

secure padlock icon in the browser address bar.
2. **Minimize Data Collection:** Minimize the amount of data collected during the checkout process to reduce the risk of data breaches and unauthorized access. Only collect essential information required to process the transaction, such as billing and shipping addresses, payment details, and contact information. Avoid storing sensitive payment information on your servers and use tokenization or third-party payment gateways to handle payment processing securely without storing credit card numbers or other sensitive data on your servers.
3. **Provide Secure Payment Options:** Offer secure payment options and integrate trusted payment gateways that comply with industry standards and security protocols to protect customer payment information. Choose payment gateways that support secure payment methods, such as tokenization, encryption, and fraud detection, to ensure that sensitive data is protected during the payment process. Display recognized payment logos and security seals to

reassure customers and instill confidence in the security of their transactions.

4. **Implement Multi-Factor Authentication:** Implement multi-factor authentication (MFA) or two-factor authentication (2FA) to add an extra layer of security to your checkout process and verify the identity of customers before completing transactions. Require customers to verify their identity using a second form of authentication, such as a one-time password (OTP) sent to their mobile device or email, in addition to entering their username and password. MFA helps prevent unauthorized access to customer accounts and reduces the risk of account takeover and fraud.

5. **Enable Address Verification:** Enable address verification services (AVS) to verify the authenticity of billing addresses provided by customers during the checkout process. AVS compares the billing address entered by the customer with the address on file with the credit card issuer to validate the transaction and reduce the risk of fraudulent transactions. Configure your payment gateway to perform AVS checks and flag transactions with mismatched or invalid addresses for further review and verification.

6. **Implement Fraud Detection Tools:** Implement fraud detection tools and

algorithms to identify and prevent fraudulent transactions in real-time. Use machine learning, artificial intelligence, and behavioral analytics to analyze transaction patterns, detect suspicious activities, and flag potentially fraudulent transactions for manual review. Configure rules and thresholds to automatically block or flag transactions that exhibit high-risk indicators, such as unusual purchase amounts, multiple failed login attempts, or suspicious IP addresses.

7. **Offer Guest Checkout Option:** Offer a guest checkout option that allows customers to complete purchases without creating an account or providing unnecessary personal information. Guest checkout reduces friction for first-time customers and encourages impulse purchases, but still, ensure that guest checkout processes are secure and compliant with data protection regulations. Provide clear instructions and guidance to guide customers through the checkout process and reassure them about the security of their transactions.

8. **Display Trust Signals:** Display trust signals and security badges prominently during the checkout process to reassure customers and build confidence in the security of their transactions. Include recognized security logos, SSL certificates,

PCI compliance badges, and trust seals from reputable organizations to indicate that your website is secure, trustworthy, and compliant with industry standards. Position trust signals strategically near the payment form or checkout button to catch customers' attention and alleviate concerns about security and privacy.

9. **Educate Customers About Security:** Educate customers about the importance of security and privacy during the checkout process to raise awareness and encourage safe online shopping practices. Provide information about the security measures in place to protect customer data, such as encryption, fraud detection, and compliance with data protection regulations. Offer tips and best practices for creating strong passwords, avoiding phishing scams, and protecting personal information to help customers safeguard their accounts and transactions.

10. **Regularly Update and Monitor:** Regularly update and monitor your checkout process and security protocols to address emerging threats, vulnerabilities, and compliance requirements. Stay informed about the latest security trends, technologies, and regulations affecting e-commerce and implement necessary updates and enhancements to maintain the integrity and

security of your checkout process. Monitor transaction logs, security alerts, and customer feedback for signs of suspicious activity or security incidents and take prompt action to investigate and mitigate potential risks.

In summary, implementing secure checkout processes is essential for protecting customer data, preventing fraud, and building trust and confidence in your e-commerce store. By using SSL encryption, minimizing data collection, providing secure payment options, implementing multi-factor authentication, enabling address verification, implementing fraud detection tools, offering guest checkout, displaying trust signals, educating customers about security, and regularly updating and monitoring security measures, you can create a secure and seamless checkout experience that instills confidence in your customers and encourages them to complete their purchases.

Chapter 6

Marketing and Promotions

Marketing and promotions play a crucial role in the success of any business, especially in the competitive landscape of the digital age. Effective marketing strategies help businesses attract, engage, and retain customers, drive sales and revenue, and build brand awareness and loyalty. In this comprehensive guide, we'll explore the key components of marketing and promotions, including developing a marketing strategy, content marketing and SEO, social media marketing, and email marketing, to help businesses reach their target audience, achieve their business goals, and stand out in the marketplace.

A. Developing a Marketing Strategy

Developing a marketing strategy is the foundation of any successful marketing campaign. A well-defined marketing strategy outlines the goals, target audience, messaging, channels, and tactics to be used to achieve desired outcomes. Here's how to develop a comprehensive marketing strategy:

1. **Define Your Goals:** Start by defining your marketing goals and objectives. What do you want to achieve with your marketing efforts? Whether it's increasing brand awareness, driving website traffic, generating leads, boosting sales, or improving customer retention, clearly define your goals to guide your strategy and measure success.
2. **Know Your Audience:** Understand your target audience's demographics, preferences, needs, and pain points to tailor your marketing messages and tactics effectively. Conduct market research, analyze customer data, and create buyer personas to identify your ideal customers and segment your audience based on factors such as age, gender, location, interests, and purchasing behavior.
3. **Identify Key Messages:** Develop key messages and value propositions that resonate with your target audience and differentiate your brand from competitors. Highlight the unique features, benefits, and value of your products or services and

communicate them clearly and consistently across all marketing channels and touchpoints.
4. **Choose Your Channels:** Select the most appropriate marketing channels and platforms to reach your target audience effectively. Consider a mix of online and offline channels, such as digital advertising, social media, content marketing, email marketing, search engine optimization (SEO), public relations, events, and traditional advertising, based on your audience's preferences, behavior, and media consumption habits.
5. **Set Your Budget:** Allocate resources and budget for your marketing initiatives based on your goals, audience size, and chosen channels. Determine how much you can afford to spend on marketing and prioritize investments in high-impact tactics and channels that offer the best return on investment (ROI) for your business.
6. **Create a Timeline:** Develop a marketing calendar or timeline outlining key activities, campaigns, and milestones to keep your marketing efforts organized and on track. Break down your strategy into

actionable steps, set deadlines, and allocate resources efficiently to ensure timely execution and delivery of marketing initiatives.

7. **Measure and Analyze Results:** Implement tracking mechanisms and analytics tools to measure the performance and effectiveness of your marketing campaigns. Monitor key performance indicators (KPIs) such as website traffic, leads generated, conversion rates, customer acquisition cost (CAC), return on ad spend (ROAS), and customer lifetime value (CLV) to evaluate the impact of your marketing efforts and identify areas for improvement.

8. **Adapt and Iterate:** Review and analyze marketing data and insights regularly to identify trends, patterns, and opportunities for optimization. Use feedback from customers, stakeholders, and team members to refine your marketing strategy, adjust tactics, and experiment with new approaches to achieve better results over time. Stay agile and responsive to changes in the market, industry, and consumer behavior to stay ahead of the competition and drive

continuous improvement in your marketing efforts.

By following these steps, businesses can develop a comprehensive marketing strategy that aligns with their goals, resonates with their target audience, and drives meaningful results across various channels and touchpoints.

B. Content Marketing and SEO

Content marketing and SEO (search engine optimization) are integral components of any digital marketing strategy. Content marketing involves creating and distributing valuable, relevant, and consistent content to attract and engage a target audience, while SEO focuses on optimizing website content and online presence to improve search engine rankings and visibility. Here's how to leverage content marketing and SEO effectively:

1. **Develop a Content Strategy:** Define your content marketing strategy by identifying your target audience, content goals, messaging, and distribution channels. Create a content calendar outlining topics, formats, and publication schedules to

ensure a consistent flow of content that addresses audience needs and aligns with business objectives.
2. **Create High-Quality Content:** Produce high-quality, relevant, and engaging content that provides value to your target audience and addresses their needs, interests, and pain points. Experiment with different content formats such as blog posts, articles, videos, infographics, podcasts, webinars, ebooks, and case studies to cater to diverse preferences and consumption habits.
3. **Optimize for SEO:** Optimize your content for search engines by incorporating relevant keywords, phrases, and topics that align with user search queries and intent. Conduct keyword research to identify high-volume, low-competition keywords related to your industry, products, and target audience, and integrate them naturally into your content, headings, titles, and meta tags to improve search engine rankings and visibility.
4. **Publish Regularly:** Consistently publish fresh, valuable content to keep your audience engaged and attract search engine traffic. Maintain

a regular posting schedule and update your website and blog with new content regularly to signal to search engines that your site is active, relevant, and authoritative. Monitor content performance and adjust your publishing frequency and cadence based on audience engagement and SEO results.
5. **Promote Across Channels:** Promote your content across various channels and platforms to maximize reach and engagement. Share your content on social media, email newsletters, industry forums, online communities, and content syndication platforms to expand your audience and drive traffic back to your website. Encourage social sharing, comments, and discussions to amplify your content's reach and visibility.
6. **Build Backlinks**: Build quality backlinks to your website from reputable and relevant sources to improve your site's authority and credibility in the eyes of search engines. Seek opportunities for guest blogging, influencer collaborations, industry partnerships, and directory listings to earn backlinks from authoritative websites and

publications. Create valuable, shareable content that naturally attracts inbound links and references from other sites.

7. **Optimize Website Structure:** Optimize your website's structure, navigation, and internal linking to improve user experience and search engine crawlability. Organize content into logical categories and subcategories, create user-friendly URLs, and use descriptive anchor text for internal links to help search engines understand the relevance and context of your content. Ensure that your website is mobile-friendly, fast-loading, and accessible to improve user engagement and search rankings.

8. **Monitor and Measure Results:** Monitor content performance and SEO metrics using analytics tools to track website traffic, keyword rankings, backlink profile, engagement metrics, and conversion rates. Analyze data regularly to identify content gaps, opportunities, and areas for improvement, and adjust your content strategy and SEO tactics accordingly to drive better results and achieve your marketing goals.

By implementing a robust content marketing strategy and SEO best practices, businesses can create valuable, discoverable content that attracts and engages their target audience, improves search engine rankings, and drives organic traffic and conversions to their website.

C. Social Media Marketing

Social media marketing is a powerful tool for businesses to connect with their audience, build brand awareness, drive website traffic, and engage with customers in real-time. With billions of active users on social media platforms, businesses can leverage social media marketing to reach and engage their target audience effectively. Here's how to harness the power of social media marketing:

1. **Define Your Objectives:** Start by defining your social media marketing objectives to clarify your goals and guide your strategy. Whether you aim to increase brand awareness, drive website traffic, generate leads, boost sales, or improve customer engagement, clearly defined objectives will help you focus your efforts and measure success effectively.

2. Know Your Audience: Understand your target audience's demographics, interests, preferences, and behavior on social media to tailor your messaging and content effectively. Conduct audience research, analyze social media insights, and create buyer personas to identify who your audience is, where they hang out online, and what content resonates with them.

3. Choose the Right Platforms: Select the most appropriate social media platforms based on your target audience, business objectives, and industry. Consider factors such as platform demographics, user engagement, content formats, and advertising options to determine which platforms align with your goals and offer the best opportunities to reach and engage your audience.

4. Create Compelling Content: Develop engaging and relevant content that captures the attention of your audience and encourages interaction and sharing. Experiment with different content formats, such as images, videos, infographics, polls, quizzes, stories, and live streams, to keep your feed diverse and engaging. Tailor your content to each platform's unique features and audience preferences to maximize engagement and impact.

5. Maintain Consistency: Maintain a consistent posting schedule to keep your audience engaged and stay top-of-mind. Create a content calendar outlining when and what type of content you'll post on each platform, and stick to it to maintain a steady stream of content. Consistency is key to building brand awareness, growing your audience, and fostering relationships with your followers over time.

6. Engage with Your Audience: Actively engage with your audience by responding to comments, messages, and mentions promptly. Foster conversations, ask questions, and encourage user-generated content to create a sense of community around your brand. Show appreciation for your followers' support, acknowledge their feedback, and address any concerns or inquiries professionally and empathetically.

7. Leverage Paid Advertising: Consider investing in paid advertising on social media platforms to extend your reach, target specific audiences, and drive measurable results. Experiment with different ad formats, targeting options, and campaign objectives to maximize your return on investment (ROI) and achieve your marketing goals. Set clear objectives, define your target audience, and allocate your budget effectively to optimize campaign performance and drive results.

8. Monitor and Analyze Performance: Monitor the performance of your social media marketing efforts using analytics tools and platform insights to track key metrics and measure success. Monitor metrics such as reach, engagement, impressions, click-through rates, conversion rates, and return on ad spend (ROAS) to evaluate the effectiveness of your campaigns and content. Use data-driven insights to identify trends, optimize performance, and inform future strategy and decision-making.

9. Stay Updated and Adapt: The social media landscape is constantly evolving, with new features, trends, and algorithms emerging regularly. Stay updated on the latest social media trends, best practices, and platform updates to adapt your strategy accordingly and capitalize on new opportunities. Experiment with new content formats, features, and strategies to keep your social media presence fresh, relevant, and engaging for your audience.

10. Build Relationships with Influencers: Collaborate with influencers, brand ambassadors, or industry experts to amplify your reach and credibility on social media. Identify influencers whose audience aligns with your target demographic and partner with them on sponsored content, co-branded campaigns, or joint promotions to reach new

audiences, increase engagement, and build brand advocacy.

By following these tips and best practices, businesses can leverage social media marketing to build meaningful connections with their audience, drive brand awareness, and achieve their marketing objectives effectively in today's digital landscape.

D. Email Marketing

Email marketing remains one of the most effective and reliable channels for reaching and engaging with your audience, nurturing leads, and driving conversions. With the ability to deliver personalized, targeted messages directly to subscribers' inboxes, email marketing allows businesses to build relationships, promote products or services, and drive desired actions. Here's how to leverage email marketing effectively:

1. Build Your Email List: Start by building a quality email list of subscribers who have opted in to receive communications from your brand. Offer incentives such as discounts, exclusive content, or freebies to encourage website visitors, social media followers, and

customers to subscribe to your email list. Use signup forms, pop-ups, landing pages, and lead magnets to capture email addresses and grow your list organically.
2. Segment Your Audience: Segment your email list based on demographic, behavioral, and psychographic factors to deliver targeted and relevant content to different segments of your audience. Divide your subscribers into groups based on criteria such as location, interests, purchase history, engagement level, and lifecycle stage to tailor your messaging and offers to their specific needs and preferences.
3. Personalize Your Emails: Personalize your email campaigns to make them more relevant and engaging for recipients. Address subscribers by name, customize subject lines and content based on their interests or past interactions with your brand, and dynamically insert personalized product recommendations, offers, or content blocks based on their preferences and behavior. Personalization increases open rates, click-through rates, and conversion rates by delivering content that

resonates with recipients on a personal level.
4. Create Compelling Content: Develop compelling and valuable content that captures recipients' attention and encourages them to take action. Craft engaging subject lines that pique curiosity and entice subscribers to open your emails. Create visually appealing and well-designed email templates that align with your brand identity and message. Include clear and compelling calls-to-action (CTAs) that prompt recipients to click, shop, sign up, or learn more.
5. Automate Email Campaigns: Implement email automation workflows to streamline your email marketing efforts and deliver timely, relevant messages to subscribers at each stage of the customer journey. Set up automated welcome emails, abandoned cart reminders, post-purchase follow-ups, re-engagement campaigns, and birthday or anniversary emails to nurture leads, drive conversions, and retain customers effectively. Use behavioral triggers and segmentation criteria to trigger automated emails based on specific actions or criteria.

6. Test and Optimize: Test different elements of your email campaigns, such as subject lines, sender names, content, CTAs, and sending times, to identify what resonates best with your audience and drives the highest engagement and conversion rates. Conduct A/B tests or multivariate tests to compare variations and determine the most effective strategies for improving open rates, click-through rates, and conversion rates. Use insights from testing to optimize your email campaigns for better performance over time.
7. Monitor Performance Metrics: Monitor key performance metrics and analytics to track the effectiveness and impact of your email marketing campaigns. Track metrics such as open rates, click-through rates, conversion rates, unsubscribe rates, bounce rates, and revenue generated to evaluate campaign performance and identify areas for improvement. Use email marketing software or analytics tools to generate reports, analyze trends, and gain insights into subscriber behavior and preferences.
8. Ensure Compliance: Ensure compliance with email marketing

regulations and best practices to maintain sender reputation, deliverability, and trust with subscribers. Familiarize yourself with laws such as the CAN-SPAM Act (in the United States) and GDPR (in the European Union) and adhere to guidelines regarding consent, permission, opt-in/opt-out mechanisms, and data protection when sending marketing emails. Obtain explicit consent from subscribers before adding them to your email list and provide clear options for unsubscribing or managing preferences.

9. Provide Value and Utility: Focus on providing value and utility to subscribers through your email marketing campaigns by delivering informative, educational, entertaining, or promotional content that addresses their needs and interests. Offer exclusive discounts, special offers, sneak peeks, product recommendations, useful tips, relevant content, and valuable resources that incentivize subscribers to engage with your emails and stay subscribed to your list.

10. Continuously Improve: Continuously monitor, analyze, and iterate on your email marketing efforts to improve performance and achieve better results over time. Regularly review campaign metrics, customer feedback, and industry trends to identify opportunities for optimization, innovation, and growth. Experiment with new tactics, strategies, and technologies to stay ahead of the curve and keep your email marketing efforts fresh, relevant, and effective in an ever-evolving landscape.

By following these strategies and best practices, businesses can harness the power of email marketing to connect with their audience, drive engagement and conversions, and achieve their marketing goals effectively and efficiently. Email marketing remains a valuable tool for building relationships, nurturing leads, and driving revenue in today's digital marketing ecosystem.

Chapter 7

Managing Finances and Operations

Managing finances and operations is essential for the success and sustainability of any business, regardless of its size or industry. Effective financial management ensures that resources are allocated efficiently, expenses are controlled, and profitability is maximized, while operational management focuses on streamlining processes, optimizing productivity, and delivering value to customers. In this comprehensive guide, we'll explore key aspects of managing finances and operations, including budgeting and financial planning, inventory management, and fulfillment and shipping, to help businesses achieve their objectives and thrive in today's competitive landscape.

A. Budgeting and Financial Planning

Budgeting and financial planning are fundamental processes that enable businesses to set financial goals, allocate resources effectively, and monitor performance against targets. By establishing a comprehensive budget and financial plan, businesses can make informed decisions, prioritize investments, and mitigate financial risks. Here's how to manage budgeting and financial planning effectively:

1. Define Financial Goals: Start by defining your financial goals and objectives, both short-term and long-term. Determine what you want to achieve financially, whether it's increasing revenue, reducing costs, improving profitability, expanding operations, or investing in growth opportunities. Align your financial goals with your overall business strategy and vision to ensure coherence and consistency.
2. Conduct Financial Analysis: Conduct a thorough analysis of your current financial situation, including revenue, expenses, cash flow, assets, liabilities, and profitability. Review historical financial data, financial statements, and performance metrics to identify trends, patterns, and areas for improvement. Use financial ratios, benchmarks, and comparisons with industry peers to assess your

financial health and performance relative to industry standards.
3. Develop a Budget: Develop a comprehensive budget that outlines your expected revenues, expenses, and cash flows for a specific period, typically a fiscal year or quarter. Estimate revenues based on sales forecasts, pricing strategies, and market trends, and budget for operating expenses, such as payroll, rent, utilities, supplies, marketing, and administrative costs. Allocate funds for capital expenditures, debt repayments, taxes, and contingencies to cover unexpected expenses or emergencies.
4. Monitor and Control Expenses: Monitor your expenses closely and control costs to ensure that they remain within budgeted limits and aligned with revenue expectations. Implement cost-saving measures, negotiate better terms with suppliers, optimize resource utilization, and eliminate unnecessary or non-essential expenses to improve profitability and cash flow. Regularly review and update your budget to reflect changes in market conditions,

business priorities, and financial performance.
5. Forecast Cash Flow: Forecast cash flow projections to anticipate inflows and outflows of cash and ensure sufficient liquidity to meet financial obligations and fund business operations. Estimate cash receipts from sales, investments, and financing activities, and project cash disbursements for expenses, purchases, debt repayments, and capital investments. Identify potential cash flow gaps or shortages and develop contingency plans to address liquidity challenges or financing needs.
6. Manage Working Capital: Manage working capital effectively to optimize liquidity, minimize financing costs, and support day-to-day operations. Monitor and manage inventory levels, accounts receivable, and accounts payable to maintain a healthy cash conversion cycle and avoid excessive tied-up capital or liquidity constraints. Implement strategies to accelerate cash inflows, such as offering discounts for early payments or incentivizing prompt invoice settlement, and optimize

payment terms with suppliers to manage cash outflows effectively.
7. Invest Wisely: Make informed investment decisions to allocate capital strategically and generate returns that align with your business goals and risk tolerance. Evaluate investment opportunities, such as expansion projects, technology upgrades, acquisitions, or market investments, based on their potential ROI, payback period, and risk profile. Diversify your investment portfolio to mitigate risk and maximize returns, and regularly review investment performance to assess effectiveness and adjust strategies as needed.
8. Seek Professional Advice: Consider seeking professional advice from financial advisors, accountants, or consultants with expertise in budgeting and financial planning. Collaborate with financial professionals to develop customized financial strategies, analyze complex financial issues, and navigate regulatory requirements or compliance challenges. Leverage their expertise and insights to optimize financial performance,

mitigate risks, and achieve your business objectives effectively.
9. Use Financial Tools and Software: Utilize financial tools and software to streamline budgeting, forecasting, and financial analysis processes and enhance decision-making capabilities. Invest in accounting software, budgeting tools, financial dashboards, and reporting systems that offer features such as real-time data visibility, customizable reporting, scenario analysis, and predictive modeling to improve financial visibility, accuracy, and efficiency.
10. Review and Adjust Regularly: Review your budget and financial plan regularly to track progress, evaluate performance against targets, and identify variances or deviations from expectations. Conduct regular budget reviews, variance analysis, and financial performance reviews to identify areas for improvement, adjust forecasts, and update strategies based on changing market dynamics, business priorities, or financial goals. Continuously iterate and refine your budgeting and financial planning processes to adapt to evolving

business needs and market conditions effectively.

By implementing these strategies and best practices, businesses can manage budgeting and financial planning effectively, optimize resource allocation, and drive financial performance and sustainability.

B. Inventory Management

Inventory management is a critical aspect of operations management that involves overseeing the sourcing, storage, tracking, and control of inventory to meet customer demand efficiently while minimizing costs and maximizing profitability. Effective inventory management ensures that businesses maintain optimal inventory levels, avoid stockouts or overstock situations, and streamline order fulfillment processes. Here's how to manage inventory effectively:

1. Conduct Demand Forecasting: Start by conducting demand forecasting to anticipate customer demand and determine optimal inventory levels for each product SKU or category. Analyze historical sales data, market trends, seasonal patterns, and customer behavior to forecast future

demand accurately. Use forecasting models, such as time series analysis, moving averages, or regression analysis, to predict demand variability and plan inventory replenishment accordingly.
2. Classify Inventory Items: Classify inventory items based on their demand variability, value, and importance to prioritize inventory management efforts and allocate resources effectively. Use ABC analysis or Pareto analysis to categorize inventory items into A, B, and C categories based on their contribution to revenue, profitability, or sales volume. Focus on managing high-value or high-demand items more closely while adopting a more relaxed approach for low-value or low-demand items.
3. Set Reorder Points and Safety Stock Levels: Set reorder points and safety stock levels for each inventory item to trigger replenishment orders and prevent stockouts. Determine the minimum inventory level at which to reorder each item, taking into account lead times, order quantities, and demand variability. Calculate safety stock levels to buffer against demand

uncertainty, supply chain disruptions, or unexpected fluctuations in demand, ensuring that you have sufficient inventory on hand to meet customer orders without delays.
4. Implement Just-in-Time (JIT) Practices: Implement just-in-time (JIT) inventory practices to minimize inventory holding costs, reduce waste, and improve operational efficiency. Adopt lean principles and practices such as kanban systems, pull-based replenishment, and demand-driven production to synchronize inventory levels with customer demand and minimize excess inventory buildup. Collaborate closely with suppliers to establish reliable and efficient supply chains that deliver materials and components on time and in the right quantities.
5. Utilize Inventory Management Systems: Implement inventory management systems and software to streamline inventory tracking, control, and replenishment processes. Invest in inventory management software that offers features such as real-time inventory visibility, barcode scanning, automatic reorder alerts, and inventory optimization tools to

improve accuracy, efficiency, and decision-making. Integrate inventory management systems with other business systems, such as point-of-sale (POS) systems, e-commerce platforms, and accounting software, to synchronize inventory data and streamline order processing and fulfillment.

6. Optimize Inventory Turnover: Focus on optimizing inventory turnover ratios to maximize inventory efficiency and minimize carrying costs. Strive to achieve a balance between maintaining adequate inventory levels to meet customer demand and minimizing excess inventory that ties up capital and storage space. Analyze inventory turnover rates, days sales of inventory (DSI), and inventory aging to identify slow-moving or obsolete items, optimize SKU assortment, and implement strategies to liquidate excess inventory or reduce carrying costs.

7. Monitor Stock Levels: Monitor stock levels regularly to track inventory levels, identify shortages or surplus, and maintain optimal inventory levels. Conduct regular physical inventory counts or cycle counts to verify stock accuracy and reconcile discrepancies between inventory records and actual inventory levels. Implement stock level alerts and automated notifications to

alert inventory managers or purchasing teams when stock levels fall below or exceed predetermined thresholds, enabling proactive inventory management and replenishment.

8. Implement Inventory Control Measures: Implement inventory control measures and best practices to prevent inventory shrinkage, theft, or loss and ensure inventory accuracy and integrity. Establish strict inventory control policies, procedures, and access controls to restrict unauthorized access to inventory storage areas and maintain chain of custody. Implement security measures such as CCTV surveillance, access controls, and inventory audits to deter theft or unauthorized removal of inventory and enforce compliance with inventory management policies.

9. Streamline Order Fulfillment: Streamline order fulfillment processes to expedite order processing, reduce lead times, and improve customer satisfaction. Optimize warehouse layout and organization to minimize picking and packing times, optimize order picking routes, and maximize storage space utilization. Implement efficient order fulfillment workflows, such as batch picking, zone picking, or wave picking, to improve order accuracy and efficiency and reduce labor costs associated with order fulfillment.

10. Continuously Improve: Continuously evaluate and improve inventory management processes, systems, and performance to adapt to changing business needs and market conditions. Monitor key performance indicators (KPIs) such as inventory turnover, stockout rates, fill rates, carrying costs, and order cycle times to measure inventory management effectiveness and identify opportunities for optimization. Solicit feedback from stakeholders, suppliers, and customers to identify pain points, bottlenecks, or inefficiencies in inventory management processes and implement corrective actions or process improvements to enhance performance and drive operational excellence.

By implementing these strategies and best practices, businesses can optimize inventory management processes, minimize costs, and improve operational efficiency and customer satisfaction. Effective inventory management is essential for ensuring that businesses maintain the right balance of inventory to meet customer demand while minimizing carrying costs and maximizing profitability.

C. Fulfillment and Shipping

Fulfillment and shipping are critical components of the supply chain that involve processing customer orders, picking, packing, and shipping products to customers in a timely and efficient manner. Effective fulfillment and shipping processes are essential for delivering a positive customer experience, minimizing shipping costs, and optimizing operational efficiency. Here's how to manage fulfillment and shipping effectively:

1. Define Order Fulfillment Process: Define and document your order fulfillment process to establish standardized procedures, workflows, and responsibilities for processing and fulfilling customer orders. Develop clear guidelines for order receipt, order processing, picking, packing, shipping, and order tracking to ensure consistency and accuracy in fulfillment operations. Map out each step of the fulfillment process and identify key touchpoints, stakeholders, and performance metrics to monitor and measure fulfillment performance.

2. Choose Shipping Carriers and Services: Choose shipping carriers and services that offer reliable delivery options, competitive rates, and tracking capabilities to meet customer expectations and shipping requirements. Evaluate shipping carriers based on factors such as transit times, delivery reliability, shipping costs, package size and weight limits, international shipping capabilities, and additional services such as insurance, tracking, and returns management. Negotiate favorable shipping rates and terms with carriers based on shipping volumes, frequency, and destination coverage to minimize shipping costs and maximize value.
3. Optimize Packaging: Optimize packaging materials, dimensions, and configurations to minimize shipping costs, protect products during transit, and optimize space utilization. Choose packaging materials that are lightweight, durable, and cost-effective, such as corrugated cardboard boxes, bubble mailers, polyethylene bags, or padded envelopes. Right-size packaging to match product dimensions and reduce

dimensional weight surcharges imposed by carriers. Use packaging design and labeling to enhance brand visibility, convey product information, and provide a positive unboxing experience for customers.
4. Automate Order Processing: Automate order processing and fulfillment tasks using order management systems, warehouse management systems (WMS), or e-commerce platforms to streamline order processing, improve accuracy, and expedite order fulfillment. Integrate order management systems with inventory management, shipping, and payment processing systems to automate order routing, inventory allocation, and shipping label generation. Implement barcode scanning, RFID technology, or pick-to-light systems to automate order picking, packing, and shipping processes and minimize manual errors and inefficiencies. Leverage automation and technology to synchronize inventory levels, track order status in real-time, and provide customers with accurate order tracking and delivery updates.

5. Implement Efficient Order Picking Strategies: Implement efficient order picking strategies and methodologies to optimize order fulfillment efficiency and minimize labor costs. Choose order picking methods such as batch picking, zone picking, wave picking, or automated picking systems based on factors such as order volume, SKU diversity, and warehouse layout. Optimize picking routes, aisle layouts, and storage configurations to minimize travel time, reduce picking errors, and maximize productivity for order pickers.

6. Offer Multiple Shipping Options: Offer customers multiple shipping options and delivery speeds to cater to their preferences, budget, and urgency. Provide standard shipping, expedited shipping, and express shipping options with varying delivery times and costs to accommodate different customer needs and delivery timelines. Partner with multiple shipping carriers or fulfillment centers to offer nationwide or international shipping coverage and provide customers with flexibility and choice in shipping methods.

7. Optimize Shipping Processes: Optimize shipping processes and workflows to streamline shipping operations, reduce transit times, and improve delivery performance. Implement efficient shipping

procedures such as batch processing, bulk shipping, or drop shipping to consolidate orders, reduce handling costs, and expedite order fulfillment. Use shipping software or platforms to compare shipping rates, print shipping labels, generate customs documentation, and schedule pickups with carriers seamlessly.

8. Provide Order Tracking and Visibility: Provide customers with order tracking and shipment visibility tools to track their orders in real-time and monitor delivery status and estimated arrival times. Integrate shipment tracking capabilities into your e-commerce website, order confirmation emails, and customer portals to provide customers with visibility into their order status and location throughout the shipping process. Enable proactive notifications and alerts to notify customers of order status updates, delivery delays, or delivery exceptions to manage customer expectations and enhance communication.

9. Streamline Returns and Exchanges: Streamline returns and exchanges processes to facilitate hassle-free returns and improve customer satisfaction. Implement a clear and transparent returns policy that outlines return eligibility, procedures, and timelines to guide customers through the returns process. Provide customers with pre-paid return

labels, return shipping instructions, and easy-to-follow return instructions to simplify the returns process and encourage repeat purchases. Automate returns processing and refunds to expedite returns handling, restocking, and customer refunds efficiently.

10. Monitor Performance and Continuously Improve: Monitor key performance indicators (KPIs) such as order fulfillment time, shipping accuracy, on-time delivery rates, shipping costs, and customer satisfaction scores to measure fulfillment and shipping performance effectively. Conduct regular performance reviews, post-mortems, and customer feedback surveys to identify areas for improvement, address pain points, and implement corrective actions to optimize fulfillment and shipping operations. Continuously iterate and improve fulfillment and shipping processes, systems, and workflows to enhance efficiency, reduce costs, and deliver superior customer experiences.

By implementing these strategies and best practices, businesses can optimize fulfillment and shipping operations, improve order accuracy and delivery performance, and enhance customer satisfaction and loyalty. Effective fulfillment and shipping are essential components of the customer experience and can significantly impact brand perception, customer retention, and long-term success in today's competitive e-commerce landscape.

Chapter 8

Scaling Your Online Business

Scaling your online business is essential for achieving sustainable growth, expanding market reach, and maximizing profitability. As your business evolves and matures, it's crucial to identify growth opportunities, optimize operations, and leverage resources effectively to scale your business successfully. In this comprehensive guide, we'll explore key strategies and best practices for scaling your online business, including identifying growth opportunities, hiring and outsourcing, and automating processes, to help you navigate the challenges and complexities of scaling in today's competitive landscape.

A. Identifying Growth Opportunities

Identifying growth opportunities is the first step in scaling your online business. Whether it's expanding into new markets, launching new products or services, or optimizing existing processes, identifying and capitalizing on growth opportunities is essential for driving sustainable business growth. Here's how to identify growth opportunities effectively:

1. Market Research: Conduct thorough market research to identify emerging trends, customer needs, and competitive dynamics in your industry. Analyze market size, growth rates, customer demographics, and purchasing behavior to identify untapped market segments, niche markets, or underserved customer needs that present growth opportunities for your business.
2. Customer Feedback: Gather feedback from existing customers through surveys, interviews, reviews, and social media interactions to understand their preferences, pain points, and expectations better. Use customer feedback to identify areas for improvement, product enhancements, or new features that can add value and drive customer satisfaction and loyalty.
3. Competitive Analysis: Analyze competitors' strategies, products, pricing, and marketing tactics to

identify gaps, weaknesses, or opportunities in the market that your business can exploit. Identify competitive advantages, unique selling propositions (USPs), or areas where you can differentiate your offerings and outperform competitors to capture market share and attract customers.
4. Industry Trends: Stay informed about industry trends, technological advancements, and market disruptions that could impact your business and present opportunities for growth. Monitor industry publications, trade journals, blogs, and forums to stay updated on emerging trends, consumer preferences, regulatory changes, and competitive developments that could influence your business strategy and growth trajectory.
5. Product Innovation: Invest in product innovation and development to introduce new products or services that address evolving customer needs, preferences, or market trends. Leverage customer insights, market research, and technology advancements to innovate and differentiate your offerings, improve

product quality, features, or performance, and stay ahead of the competition.
6. Strategic Partnerships: Explore strategic partnerships, alliances, or collaborations with complementary businesses, suppliers, distributors, or technology providers to leverage synergies, access new markets, or expand your product offerings. Identify potential partners that share your values, target audience, or strategic objectives and explore mutually beneficial opportunities for collaboration or co-branding.
7. Geographic Expansion: Consider expanding into new geographic markets or regions to reach a broader audience and tap into new customer segments or market opportunities. Evaluate market demand, regulatory requirements, cultural considerations, and competitive landscape in target markets to assess feasibility and develop entry strategies for geographic expansion.
8. Diversification: Diversify your product offerings, revenue streams, or customer base to reduce dependency on a single product or market and spread risk across multiple channels

or segments. Explore opportunities to cross-sell or upsell related products or services to existing customers or enter adjacent markets or industries that complement your core business and provide opportunities for growth.

9. Digital Marketing: Invest in digital marketing strategies such as search engine optimization (SEO), pay-per-click (PPC) advertising, content marketing, social media marketing, email marketing, and influencer partnerships to increase brand visibility, drive website traffic, and generate leads or sales. Leverage data analytics and marketing automation tools to track marketing performance, optimize campaigns, and allocate resources effectively to channels that deliver the highest ROI.

10. Customer Retention: Focus on customer retention strategies such as loyalty programs, personalized experiences, excellent customer service, and post-purchase engagement to cultivate long-term relationships with existing customers and maximize customer lifetime value (CLV). Invest in customer relationship management (CRM) systems, customer feedback

mechanisms, and customer support infrastructure to deliver exceptional customer experiences and foster customer loyalty and advocacy.

By identifying and capitalizing on growth opportunities effectively, businesses can lay the foundation for sustainable growth and expansion while mitigating risks and maximizing returns on investment.

B. Hiring and Outsourcing

Hiring and outsourcing are essential strategies for scaling your online business by accessing specialized expertise, expanding capacity, and delegating non-core functions to focus on strategic priorities. Whether it's hiring full-time employees, freelancers, contractors, or outsourcing specific tasks or functions, strategic talent acquisition and resource allocation are critical for supporting business growth. Here's how to approach hiring and outsourcing effectively:

1. Assess Organizational Needs: Evaluate your current organizational structure, capabilities, and resource requirements to identify gaps, bottlenecks, or areas where additional talent or expertise is needed to

support business growth and scalability. Determine which functions or roles are critical to your business operations and which can be outsourced or automated to streamline processes and free up internal resources.
2. Define Roles and Responsibilities: Clearly define roles, responsibilities, and expectations for each position or function within your organization to ensure alignment with business objectives, values, and culture. Develop job descriptions, performance metrics, and success criteria to communicate expectations and evaluate candidates effectively during the hiring process.
3. Recruit Top Talent: Invest in recruitment strategies and talent acquisition processes to attract, identify, and recruit top talent that aligns with your business needs, values, and culture. Leverage multiple recruitment channels, such as job boards, social media, professional networks, and recruitment agencies, to reach a diverse pool of candidates and attract candidates with the skills, experience, and attributes you're looking for.

4. Offer Competitive Compensation: Offer competitive compensation packages, including salary, benefits, incentives, and perks, to attract and retain top talent in a competitive job market. Benchmark your compensation packages against industry standards and competitor offerings to ensure that your compensation packages are competitive and aligned with market trends and candidate expectations.
5. Provide Training and Development: Invest in training, development, and onboarding programs to support employee growth and development, and equip them with the skills, knowledge, and resources needed to excel in their roles and contribute to business success. Offer orientation sessions, on-the-job training, mentorship programs, and opportunities for continuous learning and professional development to empower employees to grow, adapt, and thrive in a dynamic business environment. Provide access to online courses, workshops, certifications, and skill development programs to enhance employee capabilities and drive performance improvement.

6. Foster a Positive Work Culture: Cultivate a positive work culture that promotes transparency, collaboration, innovation, and employee engagement to attract and retain top talent and foster a productive and motivated workforce. Create a supportive work environment where employees feel valued, appreciated, and empowered to contribute their ideas, share feedback, and take ownership of their work. Encourage open communication, recognize and reward achievements, and celebrate successes to foster a sense of belonging and pride among employees.

7. Leverage Freelancers and Contractors: Utilize freelancers, contractors, or gig workers to augment your internal team and access specialized skills, expertise, or resources on a project basis. Leverage online platforms, freelance marketplaces, and talent networks to find freelancers or contractors with the skills and experience you need for specific projects or tasks. Use freelancers strategically to fill temporary or seasonal roles, tackle short-term projects, or address skill gaps without committing to long-term employment contracts.

8. Outsource Non-Core Functions: Identify non-core functions or tasks that can be outsourced to third-party service providers or agencies to streamline operations, reduce

costs, and focus internal resources on core business activities. Outsource functions such as customer support, IT services, accounting, payroll, marketing, or logistics to specialized providers or agencies that can deliver cost-effective solutions and expertise in those areas. Evaluate outsourcing partners based on their track record, capabilities, scalability, and alignment with your business objectives and values.

9. Build Remote Teams: Embrace remote work and virtual collaboration to access talent pools beyond geographical boundaries and build a distributed team of remote workers, freelancers, or contractors. Leverage communication and collaboration tools such as video conferencing, project management software, and cloud-based productivity tools to facilitate remote work and foster seamless collaboration among team members regardless of location. Implement remote work policies, guidelines, and performance metrics to support remote teams and ensure productivity, accountability, and engagement.

10. Monitor Performance and Feedback: Monitor employee performance, satisfaction, and feedback regularly to assess the effectiveness of your hiring and outsourcing strategies and identify areas for improvement or adjustment. Conduct performance

reviews, check-ins, and employee surveys to gather feedback, address concerns, and make data-driven decisions to optimize talent acquisition, retention, and engagement strategies. Use performance metrics, KPIs, and employee satisfaction scores to evaluate the impact of hiring and outsourcing initiatives on business outcomes and adjust strategies as needed to support business growth and scalability.

By adopting strategic hiring and outsourcing practices, businesses can access the talent, expertise, and resources needed to support growth and scalability effectively. Whether it's building a high-performing internal team, leveraging freelancers and contractors, or outsourcing non-core functions, strategic talent acquisition and resource allocation are critical for scaling your online business successfully.

C. Automating Processes

Automating processes is essential for scaling your online business by increasing efficiency, reducing manual workloads, and optimizing resource allocation. By automating repetitive tasks, workflows, and business processes, businesses can streamline operations, improve productivity, and focus on strategic priorities that drive growth and innovation. Here's how to automate processes effectively:

1. Identify Automation Opportunities: Identify manual, repetitive, or time-consuming tasks, workflows, or processes within your organization that can be automated to streamline operations and improve efficiency. Evaluate processes such as data entry, order processing, inventory management, customer support, marketing campaigns, and reporting for automation opportunities where technology can replace or augment human intervention.
2. Leverage Technology Solutions: Invest in technology solutions, software tools, and automation platforms that automate workflows, streamline processes, and integrate with existing systems and applications. Choose automation tools and software that align with your business needs, scalability requirements, and budget constraints. Look for features such as workflow automation, task scheduling, process orchestration, and integration

capabilities to automate end-to-end processes seamlessly.
3. Implement Workflow Automation: Implement workflow automation solutions to streamline business processes, eliminate bottlenecks, and standardize workflows across departments or functions. Use workflow automation software or business process management (BPM) platforms to design, automate, and optimize workflows for tasks such as approvals, notifications, escalations, and task assignments. Automate repetitive tasks, triggers, and decision points to reduce manual intervention and ensure consistency and efficiency in process execution.
4. Integrate Systems and Applications: Integrate disparate systems, applications, and data sources within your organization to enable seamless data exchange, collaboration, and automation across departments or functions. Use application programming interfaces (APIs), middleware, or integration platforms to connect cloud-based and on-premises systems, ERP systems, CRM platforms, e-commerce platforms, and third-party

applications to automate data synchronization, data migration, and business process integration.
5. Adopt Robotic Process Automation (RPA): Consider adopting robotic process automation (RPA) technology to automate rule-based, repetitive tasks, and processes using software robots or bots. Deploy RPA bots to perform tasks such as data entry, data validation, form processing, report generation, and invoice processing with speed, accuracy, and reliability. Use RPA tools and platforms to create, deploy, and manage bots with minimal coding or programming skills and achieve significant time and cost savings.
6. Implement Chatbots and AI Assistants: Implement chatbots and artificial intelligence (AI) assistants to automate customer interactions, support inquiries, and routine tasks through conversational interfaces such as chat, voice, or messaging platforms. Deploy chatbots for functions such as customer support, sales assistance, order tracking, appointment scheduling, and FAQ responses to provide instant, personalized, and 24/7 customer

service while reducing the workload on human agents.
7. Streamline E-commerce Operations: Streamline e-commerce operations and order fulfillment processes by automating key tasks such as order processing, inventory management, shipping, and returns processing. Integrate e-commerce platforms with inventory management systems, order management systems, and shipping carriers to automate order routing, inventory synchronization, and shipping label generation. Implement rule-based automation to manage order processing, fulfillment, and customer communication efficiently.
8. Use Marketing Automation: Leverage marketing automation tools and platforms to automate marketing campaigns, lead nurturing, and customer engagement across multiple channels such as email, social media, and digital advertising. Use marketing automation software to create, schedule, and personalize marketing campaigns, segment audiences, track customer interactions, and measure campaign performance. Implement automated

workflows for lead scoring, lead nurturing, and automated email sequences to streamline marketing operations and drive engagement and conversions.
9. **Monitor and Optimize Automation:** Monitor the performance and effectiveness of automated processes and workflows regularly to identify areas for optimization, refinement, or adjustment. Track key performance indicators (KPIs), metrics, and automation analytics to measure the impact of automation initiatives on business outcomes, such as productivity gains, cost savings, and customer satisfaction. Continuously iterate, optimize, and fine-tune automated processes based on feedback, insights, and evolving business needs to maximize ROI and achieve desired outcomes.
10. **Ensure Data Security and Compliance:** Ensure data security, privacy, and compliance when automating processes by implementing robust security measures, access controls, and data encryption mechanisms to protect sensitive information and prevent unauthorized access or data breaches.

Implement data governance policies, data retention policies, and data access controls to ensure compliance with regulatory requirements, industry standards, and data protection regulations such as GDPR, CCPA, or HIPAA. Conduct regular audits, vulnerability assessments, and security testing to identify and address security vulnerabilities or risks in automated processes and systems. Collaborate with IT security professionals, compliance officers, and legal advisors to ensure that automated processes adhere to data security and compliance standards and mitigate risks effectively.

11. Provide Training and Support: Provide training, resources, and support to employees to help them adapt to automation technologies, learn new skills, and leverage automated processes effectively. Offer training programs, workshops, and tutorials to educate employees on how to use automation tools, software platforms, or robotic systems and provide hands-on experience and practice opportunities to build confidence and proficiency. Establish helpdesk support, user guides, and troubleshooting resources to assist employees with questions, issues, or

challenges related to automation adoption and usage.

12. Foster a Culture of Innovation: Foster a culture of innovation, continuous improvement, and experimentation to encourage employees to explore new technologies, tools, and automation opportunities that can drive business growth and efficiency. Encourage cross-functional collaboration, idea sharing, and knowledge exchange among teams to identify automation opportunities, share best practices, and drive innovation across the organization. Recognize and reward employees for their contributions to process improvement, automation initiatives, and innovation efforts to reinforce a culture of innovation and excellence.

By automating processes effectively, businesses can streamline operations, improve efficiency, and scale their operations to support business growth and expansion. Whether it's automating routine tasks, optimizing workflows, or leveraging advanced technologies such as RPA or AI, automation enables businesses to operate more efficiently, reduce costs, and focus on strategic initiatives that drive long-term success and competitiveness.

In conclusion, scaling your online business requires a strategic approach to identifying growth opportunities, leveraging talent and resources effectively, and optimizing operations through automation and innovation. By adopting a holistic approach to scaling, businesses can position themselves for sustainable growth, enhance competitiveness, and achieve long-term success in today's dynamic and rapidly evolving business landscape. Through strategic planning, effective execution, and continuous improvement, businesses can navigate the challenges of scaling and unlock their full potential for growth and profitability in the digital age.

Chapter 9

Handling Challenges and Risks

In the ever-evolving landscape of business, challenges and risks are inevitable. How a business navigates through these obstacles often determines its long-term success and sustainability. From fierce competition to financial hurdles and the delicate balance of managing customer service, businesses must proactively address these challenges to thrive. In this comprehensive guide, we'll explore strategies for handling challenges and risks, focusing on dealing with competition, managing customer service, and overcoming financial hurdles.

A. Dealing with Competition

Competition is an inherent aspect of the business world. Whether you're a newcomer or an established player in your industry, navigating through competition requires strategic thinking, resilience, and adaptability. Here's how to effectively deal with competition:

1. **Know Your Competition:** Conduct thorough research to understand your competitors' strengths, weaknesses, strategies, and market positioning. Analyze their products, pricing, marketing tactics, and customer base to identify areas of differentiation and competitive advantage.
2. **Focus on Your Unique Value Proposition (UVP):** Define and communicate your unique value proposition (UVP) to differentiate your brand and offerings from competitors. Highlight what sets you apart, whether it's superior product quality, exceptional customer service, innovative features, or competitive pricing.
3. **Continuous Improvement:** Embrace a culture of continuous improvement to stay ahead of the competition. Invest in research and development, innovation, and product enhancement to deliver value-added solutions that address evolving customer needs and market trends.
4. **Build Strong Customer Relationships:** Focus on building strong, long-term relationships with your customers to foster loyalty and

reduce susceptibility to competition. Provide exceptional customer experiences, personalized service, and proactive support to delight customers and earn their trust and loyalty.
5. **Monitor and Adapt:** Stay vigilant and monitor competitive dynamics, market trends, and customer preferences to adapt your strategies and tactics accordingly. Keep a close eye on competitors' moves, new entrants, and emerging trends to anticipate threats and opportunities and adjust your approach proactively.
6. **Collaborate and Network:** Explore opportunities for collaboration, partnerships, or alliances with complementary businesses, suppliers, or industry peers to leverage synergies and expand your reach. Collaborate on joint ventures, co-marketing campaigns, or co-branded initiatives to amplify your brand presence and access new markets or customer segments.
7. **Differentiate Through Innovation:** Innovate and differentiate your offerings to stay ahead of the competition and maintain a competitive edge. Invest in research,

development, and technology to innovate new products, features, or services that address unmet customer needs or disrupt existing market norms.
8. **Agility and Flexibility:** Cultivate agility and flexibility to respond swiftly to changing market conditions, customer feedback, and competitive threats. Be willing to pivot, iterate, and experiment with new strategies, tactics, or business models to adapt to evolving dynamics and seize emerging opportunities.
9. **Focus on Customer Value:** Prioritize delivering value to your customers above all else. Focus on solving customer pain points, delivering exceptional experiences, and exceeding expectations to win customer loyalty and advocacy, regardless of competitive pressures.
10. **Maintain a Long-Term Perspective:** Keep a long-term perspective and avoid getting distracted by short-term competitive skirmishes or price wars. Focus on building sustainable competitive advantages, nurturing customer relationships, and delivering long-term value to maintain your

competitive position and resilience over time.

By adopting these strategies and maintaining a proactive, customer-centric approach, businesses can effectively navigate through competitive challenges and position themselves for long-term success and growth.

B. Managing Customer Service

Customer service is a cornerstone of business success, influencing customer satisfaction, loyalty, and advocacy. Effectively managing customer service requires a combination of empathy, responsiveness, and efficiency. Here's how to excel in managing customer service:

1. **Understand Customer Needs:** Take the time to understand your customers' needs, preferences, and pain points. Listen to their feedback, conduct surveys, and analyze customer interactions to gain insights into their expectations and experiences.
2. **Provide Prompt Responses:** Respond to customer inquiries,

requests, and complaints promptly and courteously. Aim to address customer issues and concerns in a timely manner to demonstrate responsiveness and commitment to customer satisfaction.
3. **Empower Your Team:** Empower your customer service team with the authority, resources, and training needed to resolve customer issues effectively. Provide ongoing training, coaching, and support to equip them with the skills and knowledge to deliver exceptional service experiences.
4. **Personalize Interactions:** Personalize customer interactions and communications to make customers feel valued and appreciated. Use customer data, purchase history, and preferences to tailor your interactions and recommendations to each customer's unique needs and preferences.
5. **Be Proactive:** Anticipate customer needs and proactively address potential issues or concerns before they escalate. Monitor customer feedback, social media mentions, and sentiment analysis to identify

emerging trends or patterns and take proactive measures to address them.
6. **Create Seamless Omnichannel Experiences:** Offer seamless omnichannel experiences across multiple touchpoints and channels, including phone, email, chat, social media, and in-person interactions. Ensure consistency and continuity in service delivery and communication regardless of the channel or platform used.
7. **Seek Feedback and Continuous Improvement:** Solicit feedback from customers regularly to gauge satisfaction levels, identify areas for improvement, and measure service quality. Use customer feedback surveys, Net Promoter Score (NPS) surveys, or customer satisfaction (CSAT) surveys to collect insights and prioritize improvements.
8. **Resolve Issues with Empathy and Accountability:** Handle customer complaints and issues with empathy, professionalism, and accountability. Apologize sincerely for any inconvenience or dissatisfaction, take ownership of the issue, and work towards resolving it to the customer's satisfaction.

9. **Empower Self-Service Options:** Offer self-service options and resources, such as FAQs, knowledge bases, tutorials, and online chatbots, to empower customers to find answers to their questions or resolve issues independently. Invest in user-friendly interfaces and intuitive navigation to make self-service options easily accessible and effective for customers.

10. **Measure Performance Metrics:** Track and measure key performance metrics related to customer service, such as response time, resolution time, customer satisfaction scores, and first contact resolution rates. Use data and analytics to identify trends, patterns, and areas for improvement in customer service operations.

11. **Implement a Customer-Centric Culture:** Foster a customer-centric culture within your organization by emphasizing the importance of customer satisfaction and advocacy across all levels and departments. Encourage employees to prioritize customer needs and proactively seek opportunities to enhance the customer experience.

12. **Invest in Technology:** Leverage technology solutions such as customer relationship management (CRM) systems, helpdesk software, ticketing systems, and

chatbot platforms to streamline customer service operations, automate repetitive tasks, and enhance the efficiency and effectiveness of service delivery.

13. **Offer Rewards and Incentives:** Recognize and reward outstanding customer service performance and achievements to incentivize and motivate employees to deliver exceptional service experiences. Implement reward programs, bonuses, or incentives based on customer feedback, satisfaction scores, or service excellence metrics.

14. **Continuously Innovate:** Innovate and explore new ways to enhance the customer service experience and differentiate your brand. Stay abreast of emerging trends, technologies, and best practices in customer service management and be open to experimenting with new approaches and strategies to stay ahead of the curve.

15. **Monitor Competitor Practices:** Keep an eye on competitors' customer service practices, initiatives, and innovations to benchmark your performance and identify areas for differentiation or improvement. Learn from industry leaders and disruptors in customer service excellence and adapt their strategies to suit your business context and objectives.

By implementing these strategies and best practices, businesses can elevate their customer service operations, drive customer satisfaction and loyalty, and differentiate themselves in a competitive marketplace.

C. Overcoming Financial Hurdles

Financial hurdles are a common challenge faced by businesses at various stages of their growth journey. Whether it's managing cash flow, securing funding, or navigating economic uncertainties, businesses must adopt sound financial management practices to overcome financial hurdles effectively. Here's how to address financial challenges:

1. **Develop a Comprehensive Financial Plan:** Create a comprehensive financial plan that outlines your business objectives, revenue projections, expense forecasts, and cash flow projections. Establish financial goals, targets, and milestones to guide your financial management efforts and track progress over time.
2. **Manage Cash Flow Effectively:** Cash flow management is critical for business survival and sustainability.

Monitor your cash flow closely, including incoming revenue, outgoing expenses, and working capital requirements. Implement strategies to accelerate cash inflows, such as offering discounts for early payments or incentivizing prompt invoice payments.

3. **Control Costs and Expenses:** Take proactive measures to control costs and expenses to improve profitability and preserve financial resources. Analyze your cost structure, identify areas of inefficiency or overspending, and implement cost-cutting initiatives where feasible without compromising quality or service levels.

4. **Diversify Revenue Streams:** Diversify your revenue streams to reduce dependency on a single source of income and mitigate revenue volatility. Explore opportunities to expand into new markets, launch complementary products or services, or target additional customer segments to generate alternative revenue streams and stabilize cash flow.

5. **Secure Funding and Financing:** Explore funding options and financing sources to fuel business

growth and expansion. Consider traditional financing options such as bank loans, lines of credit, or venture capital investment, as well as alternative funding sources such as crowdfunding, peer-to-peer lending, or business grants.

6. **Negotiate Favorable Terms:** Negotiate favorable terms with suppliers, vendors, creditors, and lenders to optimize cash flow management and improve financial flexibility. Negotiate extended payment terms, discounts for bulk purchases, or flexible repayment schedules to alleviate short-term cash flow pressures and improve liquidity.
7. **Monitor and Forecast Financial Performance:** Continuously monitor and analyze your financial performance against your budget, forecasts, and financial projections. Identify variances, trends, and potential risks early on and take corrective actions or adjustments to stay on track and achieve your financial goals.
8. **Build Financial Resilience:** Build financial resilience by maintaining adequate reserves, contingency funds, or emergency savings to

weather unexpected challenges or economic downturns. Establish a buffer against financial shocks and uncertainties by setting aside funds for contingencies, capital investments, or growth initiatives.
9. **Seek Professional Advice:** Seek advice and guidance from financial experts, advisors, or mentors who can provide valuable insights, expertise, and strategic guidance on financial management, planning, and decision-making. Leverage their experience and knowledge to make informed financial decisions and navigate complex financial challenges effectively.
10. **Stay Informed and Adaptive:** Stay informed about macroeconomic trends, industry dynamics, regulatory changes, and market developments that could impact your financial outlook and business operations. Be proactive and adaptive in response to changing circumstances, market conditions, and competitive pressures to maintain financial stability and resilience.

By adopting a proactive, strategic approach to financial management and leveraging sound financial practices and principles, businesses can overcome financial hurdles, sustain growth, and achieve long-term financial success and viability.

In conclusion, handling challenges and risks is an integral part of business management and leadership. By addressing competition head-on, delivering exceptional customer service, and implementing sound financial management practices, businesses can navigate through obstacles, mitigate risks, and seize opportunities for growth and success. Through resilience, adaptability, and strategic planning, businesses can overcome challenges, thrive in competitive environments, and achieve their full potential.

Chapter 10

Measuring Success and Continuous Improvement

In the dynamic landscape of business, measuring success and continuously improving performance are essential for achieving long-term growth and sustainability. By establishing key performance indicators (KPIs), analyzing data to make informed decisions, and adapting to market changes, businesses can assess their progress, identify areas for improvement, and drive ongoing innovation and excellence. In this comprehensive guide, we'll explore strategies for measuring success and continuous improvement, focusing on the importance of KPIs, data analysis, and market adaptation.

A. Key Performance Indicators (KPIs)

Key performance indicators (KPIs) are quantifiable metrics that organizations use to evaluate their success in achieving strategic objectives and operational goals. KPIs provide actionable insights into performance, help track progress over time, and enable organizations to make data-driven decisions. Here's how to establish and leverage KPIs effectively:

1. **Define Clear Objectives:** Start by defining clear and specific objectives for your business, department, or project. Identify what success looks like and establish measurable goals that align with your strategic priorities and business objectives.
2. **Identify Relevant Metrics:** Identify the key metrics and indicators that directly contribute to achieving your objectives and goals. Focus on metrics that are relevant, actionable, and aligned with your business strategy, such as revenue growth, customer retention rate, conversion rate, or employee productivity.
3. **Establish SMART KPIs:** Develop SMART (Specific, Measurable, Achievable, Relevant, Time-bound) KPIs that are well-defined, quantifiable, and achievable within a specific timeframe. Ensure that each KPI is linked to a specific objective

and provides meaningful insights into performance.

4. **Select Leading and Lagging Indicators:** Balance leading indicators, which provide early signals of future performance trends, with lagging indicators, which measure past performance outcomes. Use leading indicators to anticipate trends and proactively adjust strategies, while lagging indicators provide retrospective insights for performance evaluation.
5. **Set Benchmarks and Targets:** Establish benchmarks and performance targets for each KPI to gauge progress and measure success. Compare actual performance against targets to identify performance gaps, areas of strength, and opportunities for improvement.
6. **Monitor and Track Performance:** Implement systems and processes to monitor and track KPIs regularly. Use dashboards, scorecards, or reporting tools to visualize performance data and communicate progress effectively to stakeholders.
7. **Analyze Variance and Trends:** Analyze variance and trends in KPI data to identify patterns, anomalies,

or deviations from expected performance. Investigate the root causes of performance fluctuations and take corrective actions to address underlying issues or capitalize on opportunities.
8. **Review and Adjust KPIs:** Regularly review and adjust KPIs based on changing business priorities, market conditions, or strategic shifts. Ensure that KPIs remain relevant, meaningful, and aligned with organizational goals and objectives.
9. **Promote Accountability and Ownership:** Foster a culture of accountability and ownership around KPIs by clearly communicating expectations, responsibilities, and performance targets to employees. Empower individuals or teams to take ownership of KPIs and drive performance improvements through collaboration and innovation.
10. **Celebrate Achievements:** Celebrate achievements and milestones when KPI targets are met or exceeded. Recognize and reward individuals or teams for their contributions to achieving KPIs and driving business success.

By establishing clear objectives, selecting relevant metrics, and monitoring performance through KPIs, businesses can measure success effectively, drive continuous improvement, and achieve their strategic goals and objectives.

B. Analyzing Data and Making Informed Decisions

Data analysis plays a crucial role in measuring success and driving continuous improvement by providing valuable insights into performance, trends, and opportunities. By analyzing data effectively, businesses can identify patterns, correlations, and actionable insights to inform decision-making and optimize business processes. Here's how to analyze data and make informed decisions:

1. **Collect Relevant Data:** Start by collecting relevant data from various sources, including internal systems, customer interactions, market research, and external databases. Ensure that data is accurate, complete, and reliable to support meaningful analysis and decision-making.
2. **Define Analytical Objectives:** Clarify the objectives and questions

you seek to answer through data analysis. Identify the key insights or hypotheses you want to explore and define the scope and methodology for your analysis accordingly.
3. **Choose Appropriate Analytical Tools:** Select the appropriate analytical tools and techniques to analyze your data effectively. Depending on the nature of your data and analysis goals, choose from a range of tools such as statistical software, data visualization platforms, business intelligence (BI) tools, or machine learning algorithms.
4. **Clean and Prepare Data:** Clean and preprocess raw data to ensure accuracy, consistency, and quality before analysis. Remove duplicates, outliers, or errors, standardize data formats, and handle missing values or inconsistencies to prepare data for analysis.
5. **Explore Data Patterns and Trends:** Explore your data to identify patterns, trends, correlations, or anomalies that may provide valuable insights into performance or behavior. Use descriptive statistics, data visualization techniques, and exploratory data analysis (EDA) to

uncover hidden patterns or relationships within your data.
6. **Perform Statistical Analysis:** Conduct statistical analysis to test hypotheses, make predictions, or infer relationships between variables. Use inferential statistics, regression analysis, hypothesis testing, or predictive modeling techniques to derive actionable insights and inform decision-making based on empirical evidence.
7. **Segment and Stratify Data:** Segment your data into meaningful groups or segments based on relevant criteria such as customer demographics, geographic location, purchase behavior, or product preferences. Stratify data to analyze performance variations across different segments and identify opportunities for targeted interventions or personalized strategies.
8. **Benchmark and Compare Performance:** Benchmark your performance against industry standards, peer benchmarks, or historical data to assess relative performance and identify areas of strength or weakness. Compare

performance metrics, KPIs, or benchmarks to track progress over time and measure improvement against targets.
9. **Generate Actionable Insights:** Translate data insights into actionable recommendations or strategies that drive business improvement or innovation. Identify opportunities for optimization, cost savings, revenue growth, or process efficiencies based on data-driven insights and prioritize initiatives based on their potential impact and feasibility.
10. **Iterate and Refine Analysis:** Continuously iterate and refine your data analysis approach based on feedback, results, and evolving business needs. Experiment with different analytical techniques, data sources, or models to improve the accuracy, robustness, and relevance of your analysis over time.

By analyzing data effectively and making informed decisions, businesses can gain valuable insights, optimize performance, and drive continuous improvement across all aspects of their operations. Data-driven decision-making enables businesses to identify opportunities, mitigate risks, and optimize processes to achieve their strategic objectives and deliver value to stakeholders.

C. Adapting to Market Changes

In today's fast-paced and volatile business environment, adaptation is key to survival and success. Market changes, including shifts in consumer preferences, technological advancements, regulatory developments, and competitive dynamics, can present both opportunities and challenges for businesses. Here's how to adapt to market changes effectively:

1. **Stay Informed and Aware:** Stay informed about market trends, industry developments, and emerging technologies that could impact your business. Monitor industry publications, market research reports, and competitor activities to stay ahead of the curve and anticipate changes in the market landscape.
2. **Conduct Market Research:** Conduct regular market research to understand evolving customer needs, preferences, and behaviors. Gather insights through surveys, focus groups, interviews, and social

listening to identify emerging trends, market gaps, and opportunities for innovation.
3. **Monitor Competitive Landscape:** Keep a close eye on competitors' strategies, product offerings, pricing, and marketing initiatives to understand their positioning and identify potential threats or opportunities. Benchmark your performance against competitors and adjust your strategies accordingly to maintain competitiveness.
4. **Adapt Product and Service Offerings:** Continuously evaluate and refine your product and service offerings to meet changing customer demands and market trends. Innovate new products, features, or solutions that address emerging needs or capitalize on untapped market opportunities.
5. **Embrace Technological Advancements:** Embrace technological advancements and digital innovations to enhance your business processes, improve efficiency, and deliver superior customer experiences. Invest in technologies such as artificial intelligence, machine learning, data

analytics, cloud computing, and automation to stay competitive and future-proof your business.
6. **Anticipate Regulatory Changes:** Stay abreast of regulatory developments and compliance requirements that impact your industry or operations. Anticipate regulatory changes and proactively adapt your policies, processes, and practices to ensure compliance and mitigate regulatory risks.
7. **Flexibility and Agility:** Cultivate flexibility and agility within your organization to respond swiftly to market changes and customer feedback. Empower employees to make decisions autonomously, experiment with new ideas, and iterate on strategies based on real-time insights and feedback.
8. **Customer-Centric Approach:** Prioritize customer-centricity in your business strategies and operations to align with evolving customer preferences and expectations. Listen to customer feedback, solicit input, and co-create solutions with customers to ensure that your offerings remain relevant and valuable.

9. **Strategic Partnerships and Alliances:** Explore strategic partnerships, alliances, or collaborations with complementary businesses, suppliers, or industry stakeholders to leverage synergies and access new markets or capabilities. Collaborate on joint ventures, co-marketing campaigns, or research initiatives to expand your reach and diversify your offerings.
10. **Risk Management and Contingency Planning:** Develop risk management strategies and contingency plans to mitigate the impact of market uncertainties, disruptions, or crises. Identify potential risks, assess their likelihood and impact, and develop proactive measures to minimize exposure and safeguard business continuity.
11. **Monitor and Evaluate Performance:** Continuously monitor and evaluate your performance against key metrics, objectives, and targets to assess the effectiveness of your adaptation strategies. Measure the impact of market changes on your business outcomes and adjust your strategies as needed to optimize

performance and capitalize on opportunities.

By adapting to market changes proactively and strategically, businesses can position themselves for long-term success, resilience, and growth in an ever-changing business landscape.

In conclusion, measuring success and driving continuous improvement require a proactive and strategic approach that encompasses establishing KPIs, analyzing data, and adapting to market changes. By setting clear objectives, leveraging data-driven insights, and staying agile and responsive to market dynamics, businesses can optimize performance, mitigate risks, and achieve sustainable growth and competitiveness. Through a commitment to excellence, innovation, and adaptation, businesses can thrive amidst uncertainty and complexity, delivering value to customers, stakeholders, and society as a whole.

Chapter 11

Conclusion

In the journey of starting and growing a successful online business from scratch, entrepreneurs face a multitude of challenges, uncertainties, and opportunities. From understanding the online business landscape to planning, building, marketing, and scaling their ventures, the path to success is paved with dedication, resilience, and strategic decision-making. As we conclude this comprehensive guide, let's recap the key points discussed throughout this book and offer encouragement and final words of advice to aspiring entrepreneurs.

A. Recap of Key Points

Throughout this book, we've covered a wide range of topics aimed at guiding you through the process of starting and growing a successful online business from scratch. Here's a recap of the key points discussed:

1. **Understanding the Online Business Landscape:** We explored the different types of online businesses, the importance of market research

and niche identification, and strategies for analyzing competitors to gain a competitive edge.
2. **Planning Your Online Business:** We discussed the significance of defining your unique selling proposition (USP), crafting a business plan, and setting goals and milestones to guide your business growth.
3. **Building Your Online Presence:** We highlighted the importance of choosing the right domain name, creating a professional website, and establishing social media profiles to enhance your online visibility and credibility.
4. **Setting Up Your E-commerce Infrastructure:** We delved into selecting the right e-commerce platform, setting up payment gateways, and implementing secure checkout processes to facilitate seamless online transactions.
5. **Marketing and Promotions:** We explored strategies for developing a marketing strategy, leveraging content marketing and SEO, harnessing the power of social media marketing, and utilizing email marketing to engage and convert customers.

6. **Managing Finances and Operations:** We discussed the importance of budgeting and financial planning, effective inventory management, and efficient fulfillment and shipping processes to ensure the smooth operation of your online business.
7. **Scaling Your Online Business:** We examined strategies for identifying growth opportunities, hiring and outsourcing effectively, and automating processes to scale your online business and achieve long-term success.
8. **Handling Challenges and Risks:** We addressed common challenges such as dealing with competition, managing customer service, and overcoming financial hurdles, offering strategies for navigating through obstacles and mitigating risks effectively.
9. **Measuring Success and Continuous Improvement:** We discussed the significance of establishing key performance indicators (KPIs), analyzing data to make informed decisions, and adapting to market changes to drive ongoing innovation and excellence.

Throughout each of these topics, the underlying theme has been one of perseverance, adaptability, and a customer-centric approach. By focusing on delivering value to customers, leveraging data-driven insights, and staying agile in the face of challenges, entrepreneurs can build resilient and thriving online businesses.

B. Encouragement and Final Words of Advice

As you embark on your journey to start and grow a successful online business, remember that challenges are inevitable, but so are opportunities. Stay focused on your vision, persevere through setbacks, and continuously seek ways to improve and innovate. Here are some final words of encouragement and advice:

1. **Believe in Yourself:** Believe in your vision and capabilities as an entrepreneur. Trust your instincts, but also be open to feedback and learning from experience.
2. **Stay Customer-Centric:** Put your customers at the center of everything you do. Listen to their feedback, anticipate their needs, and strive to

exceed their expectations at every touchpoint.
3. **Embrace Continuous Learning:** The world of online business is constantly evolving. Stay curious, stay informed, and never stop learning. Keep abreast of industry trends, emerging technologies, and best practices to stay ahead of the curve.
4. **Build a Strong Support Network:** Surround yourself with mentors, advisors, and peers who can offer guidance, support, and inspiration along the way. Seek out networking opportunities and connect with like-minded individuals who share your passion for entrepreneurship.
5. **Be Resilient:** Entrepreneurship is a journey filled with ups and downs. Be resilient in the face of adversity, learn from failure, and use setbacks as opportunities for growth and improvement.
6. **Celebrate Milestones:** Take the time to celebrate your achievements, no matter how small. Milestones are markers of progress and deserve to be acknowledged and celebrated.
7. **Give Back:** As you achieve success in your online business, remember to

give back to your community and society. Use your platform and resources to make a positive impact and contribute to causes you believe in.

Starting and growing a successful online business is a challenging yet rewarding endeavor. It requires dedication, perseverance, and a willingness to adapt to changing circumstances. By following the strategies and principles outlined in this book, you can increase your chances of success and build a thriving online venture that makes a meaningful impact in the lives of your customers and beyond.

As you embark on this exciting journey, remember that the most fulfilling rewards often come from overcoming obstacles, pushing past your comfort zone, and realizing your full potential as an entrepreneur. With determination, passion, and a commitment to excellence, you have the power to turn your dreams into reality and create a lasting legacy in the digital marketplace.

Wishing you all the best on your entrepreneurial journey. Go forth with confidence, courage, and conviction, and may your online business venture be a beacon of success and inspiration to others.

End of Conclusion

Chapter 12
Additional Resources

As you embark on your journey to start and grow a successful online business, having access to the right tools, resources, and information can make a significant difference in your success. In this section, we'll provide a curated list of recommended tools and software, further reading and references to deepen your knowledge, and a glossary of terms to clarify key concepts and terminology.

A. Recommended Tools and Software

1. **Website Builders:**
   - WordPress: A versatile and customizable platform for building websites and blogs.
   - Wix: An intuitive website builder with drag-and-drop functionality and customizable templates.
   - Shopify: A leading e-commerce platform for

creating online stores and selling products.
2. **E-commerce Platforms:**
   - Shopify: A comprehensive e-commerce solution with features for inventory management, payment processing, and marketing.
   - WooCommerce: A WordPress plugin that allows you to turn your website into a fully functional online store.
   - BigCommerce: An all-in-one e-commerce platform with built-in features for selling products online.
3. **Digital Marketing Tools:**
   - Google Analytics: A powerful analytics platform for tracking website traffic, user behavior, and conversion rates.
   - Mailchimp: An email marketing platform for creating and sending targeted email campaigns to engage customers.
   - SEMrush: A suite of SEO and digital marketing tools for keyword research,

competitive analysis, and site audit.
4. **Social Media Management:**
    - Hootsuite: A social media management platform for scheduling posts, engaging with followers, and analyzing performance.
    - Buffer: A social media scheduling tool that allows you to plan and publish content across multiple platforms.
    - Sprout Social: A comprehensive social media management and analytics platform for businesses of all sizes.
5. **Customer Relationship Management (CRM):**
    - Salesforce: A cloud-based CRM platform with tools for sales, marketing, customer service, and analytics.
    - HubSpot CRM: A free CRM software with features for managing contacts, deals, and tasks, as well as email tracking and automation.
    - Zoho CRM: An affordable CRM solution with modules

for sales automation, marketing automation, and customer support.
6. **Project Management:**
    - Asana: A flexible project management tool for organizing tasks, assigning responsibilities, and tracking progress.
    - Trello: A visual project management tool that uses boards, lists, and cards to organize tasks and collaborate with team members.
    - Monday.com: A customizable project management platform with features for workflow automation, task tracking, and team collaboration.
7. **Accounting and Finance:**
    - QuickBooks: A leading accounting software for small businesses, with features for invoicing, expense tracking, and financial reporting.
    - Xero: An online accounting software that simplifies financial management with tools for invoicing, payroll, and bank reconciliation.

- FreshBooks: A cloud-based accounting solution with features for time tracking, project management, and client invoicing.
8. **Customer Support and Helpdesk:**
    - Zendesk: A customer service software with features for ticket management, live chat support, and knowledge base creation.
    - Freshdesk: A helpdesk software that streamlines customer support operations with ticketing, automation, and self-service options.
    - Intercom: A customer messaging platform that enables personalized communication and engagement across multiple channels.
9. **Analytics and Data Visualization:**
    - Tableau: A powerful data visualization tool for creating interactive dashboards, reports, and visualizations from multiple data sources.
    - Google Data Studio: A free data visualization tool that allows you to create

- customizable reports and dashboards using data from Google Analytics, Google Ads, and other sources.
  - Power BI: A business analytics platform that enables users to visualize data, share insights, and make data-driven decisions.
10. **Cybersecurity and Data Protection:**
    - LastPass: A password management tool that securely stores and manages passwords for websites and applications.
    - McAfee: A comprehensive cybersecurity solution with antivirus, firewall, and identity theft protection features.
    - Norton Security: An antivirus and internet security suite that protects against malware, viruses, and online threats.

These recommended tools and software can help streamline your business operations, improve efficiency, and drive growth. However, it's essential to evaluate your specific needs and budget before selecting the right tools for your online business.

B. Further Reading and References

1. Books:
   - "The Lean Startup" by Eric Ries: Learn how to build a successful startup by adopting a lean and iterative approach to product development and customer validation.
   - "E-Myth Revisited" by Michael E. Gerber: Discover the myths and realities of entrepreneurship and learn how to build a business that works without you.
   - "Hooked: How to Build Habit-Forming Products" by Nir Eyal: Understand the psychology behind habit-forming products and learn how to create products that engage and retain customers.
2. Online Courses:
   - Coursera: Explore online courses on entrepreneurship, digital marketing, e-

commerce, and business management from top universities and institutions.
- Udemy: Enroll in courses on topics such as website development, SEO, social media marketing, and business strategy taught by industry experts and practitioners.
- LinkedIn Learning: Access a wide range of video tutorials and courses on business skills, leadership, and technology to enhance your knowledge and expertise.

3. Blogs and Websites:
   - Entrepreneur: Read articles and insights on entrepreneurship, startups, and business innovation from leading experts and thought leaders.
   - Shopify Blog: Explore guides, case studies, and tips on e-commerce, marketing, and entrepreneurship from the Shopify team and industry experts.
   - Neil Patel: Visit Neil Patel's blog for actionable insights

and strategies on digital marketing, SEO, content marketing, and online business growth.
4. Podcasts:
    - "The Tim Ferriss Show": Listen to interviews with top performers from various industries, including entrepreneurship, business, health, and productivity.
    - "How I Built This": Hear stories of successful entrepreneurs and business founders as they share their journeys of building and scaling iconic companies.
    - "Marketing School": Tune in to short, daily episodes hosted by Neil Patel and Eric Siu, covering actionable marketing insights and strategies for entrepreneurs.
5. Online Communities:
    - Reddit: Join communities such as r/Entrepreneur, r/Startups, and r/E-commerce to connect with fellow entrepreneurs, share experiences, and seek advice

- on building and growing online businesses.
  - LinkedIn Groups: Participate in LinkedIn Groups focused on entrepreneurship, digital marketing, and e-commerce to network with professionals, share knowledge, and learn from industry peers.

These further reading and references provide valuable insights, tips, and resources to help you deepen your knowledge and skills in entrepreneurship, online business, and digital marketing.

C. Glossary of Terms

1. **E-commerce:** Electronic commerce, or the buying and selling of goods and services over the internet.
2. **SEO (Search Engine Optimization):** The process of optimizing a website to rank higher in search engine results pages (SERPs) and increase organic traffic.
3. **USP (Unique Selling Proposition):** The unique feature or benefit that sets a product or service apart from competitors and appeals to customers.

4. **CRM (Customer Relationship Management):** A strategy and software system for managing interactions and relationships with customers and prospects.

5. **ROI (Return on Investment):** A measure of the profitability of an investment, calculated as the ratio of net profit to the initial investment cost.

6. **KPI (Key Performance Indicator):** A quantifiable metric used to evaluate the success of an organization, department, or specific activity in achieving its objectives.

7. **B2B (Business-to-Business):** A type of commerce where businesses sell products or services to other businesses rather than to consumers.

8. **B2C (Business-to-Consumer):** A type of commerce where businesses sell products or services directly to consumers.

9. **Conversion Rate:** The percentage of website visitors who take a desired action, such as making a purchase, signing up for a newsletter, or filling out a contact form.

10. **Lead Generation:** The process of attracting and converting potential customers (leads) into interested prospects for a product or service.

11. **Niche Market:** A specialized segment of the market focused on a specific product, service, or customer demographic.

12. **SaaS (Software as a Service):** A software delivery model where software is hosted on the cloud and accessed via the internet on a subscription basis.
13. **ROI (Return on Investment):** A measure of the profitability of an investment, calculated as the ratio of net profit to the initial investment cost.
14. **Content Marketing:** A marketing strategy focused on creating and distributing valuable, relevant, and consistent content to attract and engage a target audience.
15. **Fulfillment:** The process of receiving, processing, and delivering orders to customers, often involving inventory management and shipping logistics.
16. **Dropshipping:** A retail fulfillment method where a store doesn't keep the products it sells in stock. Instead, when a store sells a product, it purchases the item from a third party and has it shipped directly to the customer.
17. **SMM (Social Media Marketing):** The use of social media platforms and websites to promote a product or service and engage with customers.
18. **SSL (Secure Sockets Layer):** A security protocol that encrypts data transmitted between a user's browser and a website to protect sensitive information such

as passwords, credit card numbers, and personal details.

19. **API (Application Programming Interface):** A set of rules and protocols that allows different software applications to communicate and share data with each other.

20. **Cybersecurity:** The practice of protecting computer systems, networks, and data from cyber threats such as hacking, malware, and unauthorized access.

This glossary of terms provides definitions for common terms and concepts related to online business, e-commerce, digital marketing, and technology. Familiarizing yourself with these terms can help you better understand the discussions and resources in the field of online entrepreneurship.

As you continue your journey in building and growing your online business, leverage these additional resources to enhance your knowledge, skills, and capabilities. Whether you're looking for tools to streamline your operations, seeking further insights from expert authors and thought leaders, or clarifying key concepts through a glossary of terms, these resources can serve as valuable assets in your entrepreneurial toolkit.

Remember that entrepreneurship is a journey of continuous learning, adaptation, and growth. Stay curious, stay motivated, and never stop striving for excellence in pursuit of your online business goals.

End of Additional Resources

Book description

"Embark on the journey of launching and growing your own online business with our comprehensive guide, 'From Scratch to Success: A Blueprint for Building Your Online Empire.' Whether you're a seasoned entrepreneur or a newcomer to the world of e-commerce, this book offers invaluable insights, practical strategies, and actionable advice to help you navigate the complexities of the digital marketplace.

From understanding the fundamentals of online business and identifying lucrative niches to crafting a compelling brand and leveraging digital marketing channels, each chapter is packed with expert guidance and real-world examples to empower you on your entrepreneurial journey. Learn how to build a professional website, optimize your online presence, and implement effective e-commerce strategies to attract customers and drive sales.

With a focus on practicality and results, 'From Scratch to Success' equips you with the tools, resources, and mindset needed to turn your online business dreams into reality. Whether you're launching a side hustle or aiming for global domination, this book is your roadmap to online success."

www.ingramcontent.com/pod-product-compliance
Lightning Source LLC
Chambersburg PA
CBHW071459220526
45472CB00003B/852